This book is dedicated
to kindness to horses, both
large and small.

1,001
REASONS TO LOVE™
HORSES

SHERI SEGGERMAN & MARY TIEGREEN

STEWART, TABORI & CHANG
NEW YORK

Published in 2005 by
Stewart, Tabori & Chang
115 West 18th Street
New York, NY 10011
www.abramsbooks.com

Canadian Distribution:
Canadian Manda Group
One Atlantic Avenue, Suite 105
Toronto, Ontario, M6K 3E7
Canada

Library of Congress Cataloging-in-Publication Data

Seggerman, Sheri.
  1,001 reasons to love horses / Sheri Seggerman & Mary Tiegreen.
    p. cm.
  ISBN 1-58479-400-3
  1. Horses--Miscellanea. I. Title: One thousand one reasons to love horses. II. Tiegreen, Mary. III. Title.

SF285.S358 2005
636.1--dc22   2004023518

1,001 Reasons to Love Horses is a book in the
1,001 REASONS TO LOVE™ Series.

1,001 REASONS TO LOVE™ is a trademark of Mary Tiegreen
and Hubert Pedroli.

Printed in China

10 9 8 7 6 5 4 3 2 1

First Printing

Stewart, Tabori & Chang is a subsidiary of

LA MARTINIÈRE
GROUPE

INTRODUCTION

Some people are just born horse crazy. I was one of the lucky ones. Perhaps it's in the genes, a trait inherited from my grandmother, who told me stories of her adventures on her horse, Toots. There wasn't a day of my childhood that I didn't long for a horse: I can remember slapping my thigh and cantering, whinnying, across the backyard. My bedroom shelves were filled with horse books and china horse figurines. My bulletin board was covered with pictures of my future horse and drawings of my fantasy steed. Every toy horse had a name, and I bid each one goodnight as I fell asleep.

Then, miraculously, after ten years of hard work wishing on stars, birthday candles, and white horses, my parents gave me Sugarfoot. Sugarfoot: the essence of the Black Stallion, Flicka, and Misty of Chincoteague combined in one small, black horse with a crooked blaze, one white stocking, a kind eye, and the patience of a saint.

Sugarfoot was my best friend. He knew all my secrets and dreams. He knew that I sang a little out of tune, often didn't comb my hair, and talked too much. I knew that he sometimes liked to buck, hated to cross bridges, and loved to roll in the river. We each seemed to accept these traits

— LUCY —

in one another. We spent years together, roaming county roads and farmer's fields. Just to think about those rides— the solitude, the quiet lanes, the draping elms, my good fortune—makes me realize how indebted I am to that horse.

For many years after leaving home I didn't have a horse of my own, but I never stopped wanting one. Now I have Lucy, a grey Percheron/cross mare who has unleashed my childhood passion for horses. Now my shelves are once again filled with horse books, and my portfolio is filled with my own photographs of horses and horse people. Through lessons, travel, and endless horse talk with friends, I have dipped into every avenue of horse experience I can find, from dressage to horseracing, from hippotherapy to horse whispering.

When Mary Tiegreen asked me to co-write this book I thought, I have 1,001 reasons to love Lucy alone! The challenge was to describe as much of equine/human relationships as possible. For me, this was a chance to travel even farther on a lifelong quest. But one reason is all I really need, and she's nickering in the paddock right now, hoping for a carrot.

—Sheri Seggerman
Iowa City, 2004

A lovely horse is always an experience....
It is an emotional experience of the
kind that is spoiled by words.

—Beryl Markham

1
Learning the secret language
of the horse

Love at First Sight

Thou art a creature without equal—for thou
flyest without wings and conquerest
without sword.
—The Koran

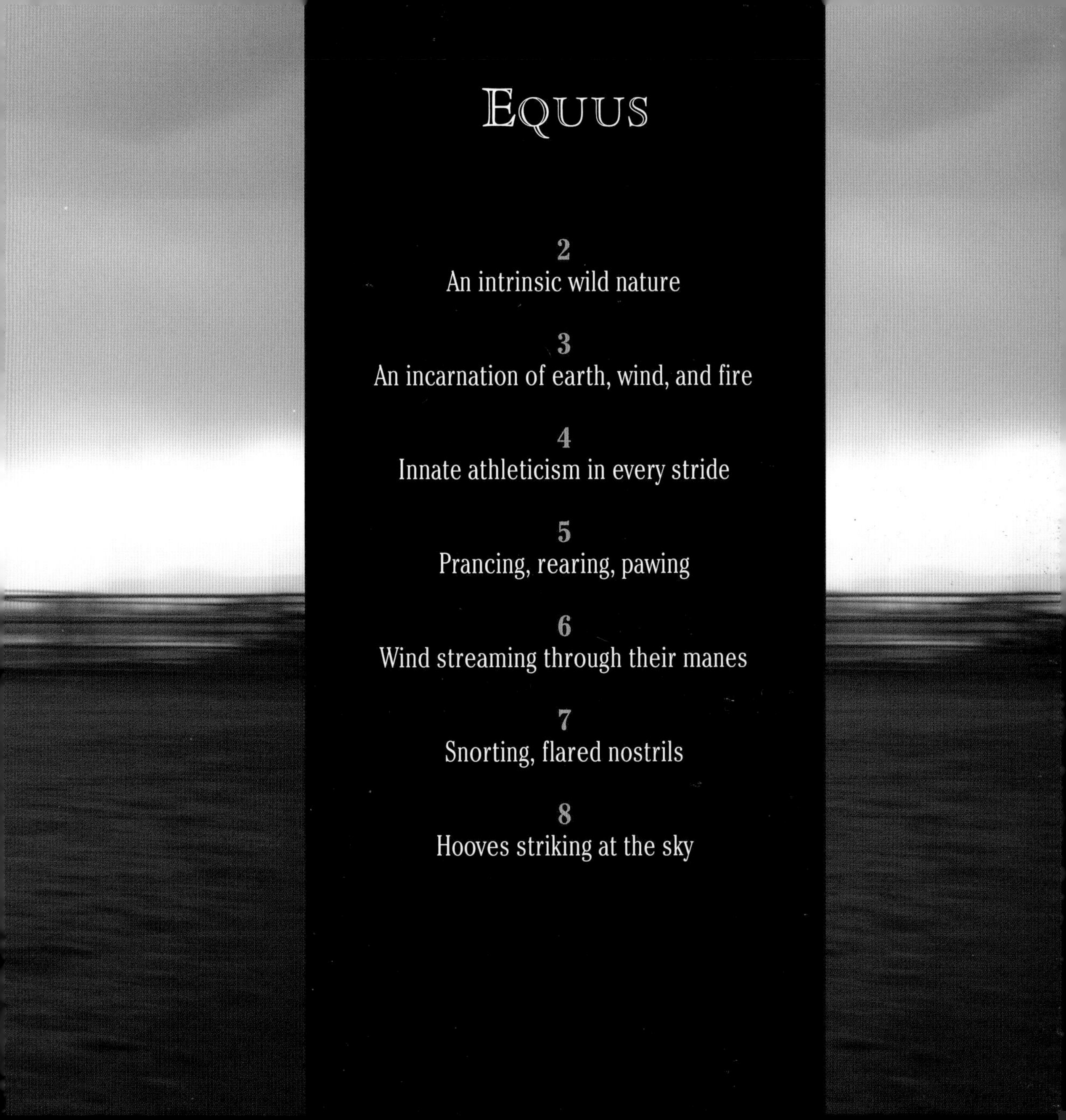

EQUUS

2

An intrinsic wild nature

3

An incarnation of earth, wind, and fire

4

Innate athleticism in every stride

5

Prancing, rearing, pawing

6

Wind streaming through their manes

7

Snorting, flared nostrils

8

Hooves striking at the sky

9
Haughtily arched necks

10
A burnished, glossy coat

11
The bone structure of
equine royalty

12
Wide-set eyes

13
Flickering, highly-attuned ears

14
Proud posture

15
A strutting, boastful style

16
Skin so fine and sensitive,
it ripples under a
light touch

35
Soft lips, soft muzzles

36
Centuries of
wisdom in a dark eye

48
A colt's untameable mane

58
The beauty of a perfect star

59
The simple pleasure of frolicking

60
Wild, rapturous gallops

61
Coy and playful trots

62
Peaceful, slow-paced ambles

63
Spirited leaps and snorts

64
Running just for pleasure

65
Bucking, kicking play

66
Spooking, spinning, fleeing

67
Lounging in the sun

85
The bonds of friendship
in a herd

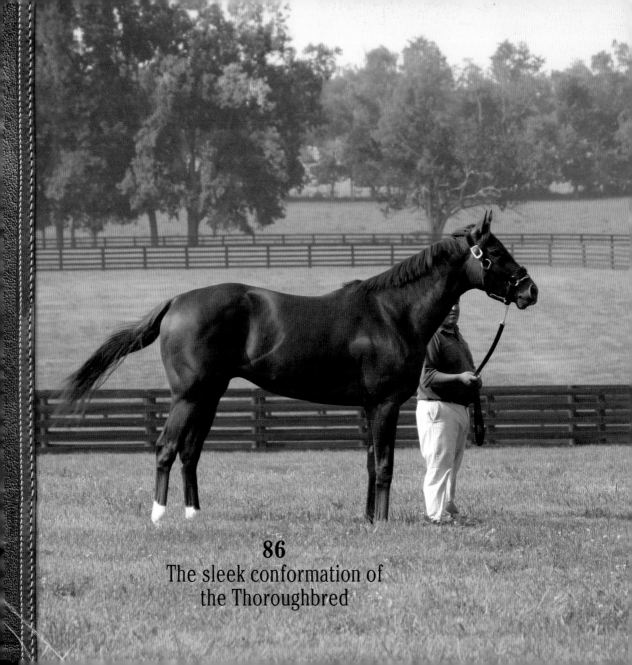

86
The sleek conformation of
the Thoroughbred

Smarty Jones at Three Chimneys,
Midway, Kentucky

87 A racing standardbred's furious, cadenced pace

88 An Appaloosa's wild eye and distinctive, splashy spots

89 A quarter horse's powerful sprint and spin

90 The Shetland pony's endearing stubbornness

91 The flamenco-like tempo of a Paso Fino's smooth-gaited step

92 A Tennessee Walking Horse's elongated, running walk

93 The silver mane and tail and chocolate coat of a Rocky Mountain horse

94 Flamboyant, jet-black feathers swirling in a Friesian's high-stepping trot

95 The easy-chair comfort of a Percheron's broad back

96 The slow, syncopated gait of a stylish Missouri Fox Trotter

The thick-coated
Icelandic horse,
friendly and stoic

98
The Belgian, America's favorite draft horse

99
The regal white Lipizzan
stallion, with his "airs
above the ground"

109
The desert-born Arabian's
elegant, small head

110
A Western pinto's natural flair

111
The rugged, wild
American mustang

116
Talking to the horse you ride
on the carousel

117
Wearing a locket that holds a
picture of a horse

118
Galloping on your rocking horse to the call of the hounds

119
Having a stick horse that runs faster
than the rest

120
Falling asleep in a herd of
stuffed horses

121 Covering the walls of your room with photos of your future horses

122 Jumping your Breyer horses over fences of chopsticks and glue

123 Giving a snort and a whinny as you gallop to your mother's call for dinner

124 Thumbing through your dog-eared copy of *The Giant Book of Horses*

125 Riding in the backseat of the car counting horses while your brother counts sports cars

126 Going to the library and checking out *Misty of Chincoteague*

127 Deciding to be a veterinarian when you grow up

128 Spending hours on the Internet looking at horses for sale

129 Going to pony camp

130 Cheering out loud, "Go, Biscuit!" while watching the match race

131
Making friends at the
local stable

Why i love horses

by isabel cody age 5

Because their manes are soft and smooth

Because they have pretty hooves

Because they love carrots

Because they're so beautiful

Because they eat their greens,
which makes them nice and healthy

Because when they run they look like
they're flying with the wind

Because they look funny when they are wearing glasses

Because they live on farms and have
other animal friends

Because they can swat flies with their tails

Because when i sit on a horse i feel like a princess

All horses deserve, at least
once in their lives, to be loved
by a little girl.

Nan and Kris on Lucky

Getting to sit on your cousin's pony, Spot

145 Finishing your fifth horse paint-by-number painting

146 Covering your notebook with horse stickers

147 Tracing horses from *Draw Horses with Sam Savitt*

148 Wearing your favorite Spirit T-shirt

149 Willing to clean a stall, but not your room

150 Hoping the Pie wins the Grand National each time you watch the movie

151 Working out whether your backyard is big enough to keep a pony in

152 Planning to convert the garage into a stable

153 Crying while reading *Black Beauty*

154 Having an imaginary horse that grazes in your room

155 Braiding the manes of your stuffed horses

156 Worrying about the ponies in the circular pony ride

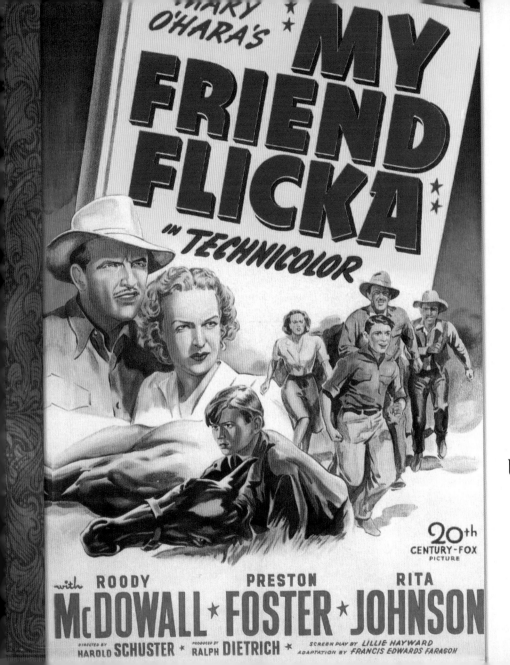

157
Understanding
why Ken
McLaughlin
chose Flicka

What Being Alive Meant

Rocket's colt—a yearling, a filly—and *his own*. He hadn't had to choose one at all. She had come to him. His own because of that second's cry for help that had come from her eyes to his; his own because of her wild beauty and speed, his own because his heart burned within him at the sight and thought of her: his own because—well, just his own . . .

No dream he had ever had, no imagination of adventure or triumph could touch this moment. He felt as if he had burst out of his old self and was something entirely new—and that the world had burst into something new too. So this was it—this was what being alive meant—Oh, my filly, my filly, my beautiful filly. . . ."

—Mary O'Hara, *My Friend Flicka*

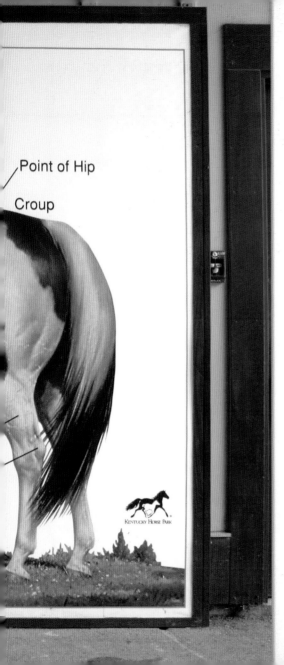

Point of Hip

Croup

Kentucky Horse Park

170 Memorizing all the words from the Anatomy of the Horse chart

171 Believing that if you were National Velvet, you wouldn't faint at the end of the race

172 Winding your jump rope around a chair as reins and practicing "throwing it away"

173 Feeling the need for a pony like a stomachache

174 Naming your bicycle Thunderbolt

175 Asking your grandpa to tell you about the workhorse Nellie

176 Wishing Henry Ford had never invented the car

177 Pretending to be Alex Ramsey in *The Black Stallion*

178 Reciting all the Triple Crown winners from memory

179 Learning the difference between a chestnut and a bay

180 Knowing that every horse you meet is the horse for you

Once You Are Real

The Skin Horse had lived longer in the nursery than any of the others. He was so old that his brown coat was bald in patches and showed the seams underneath, and most of the hairs in his tail had been pulled out to string bead necklaces. He was wise, for he had seen a long succession of mechanical toys arrive to boast and swagger, and by-and-by break their mainsprings and pass away, and he knew that they were only toys, and would never turn into anything else. For nursery magic is very strange and wonderful, and only those playthings that are old and wise and experienced like the Skin Horse understand all about it.

"What is REAL?" asked the Rabbit one day, when they were lying side by side near the nursery fender, before Nana came to tidy the room. "Does it mean having things that buzz inside you and a stick-out handle?"

"Real isn't how you are made," said the Skin Horse. "It's something that happens to you. When a child loves you for a long, long time, not just to play with, but REALLY loves you, then you become Real."

"Does it hurt?" asked the Rabbit.

"Sometimes," said the Skin Horse, for he was always truthful. "When you are Real you don't mind being hurt."

"Does it happen all at once, like being wound up," he asked, "or bit by bit?"

"It doesn't happen all at once," said the Skin Horse. "You become. It takes a long time. That's why it doesn't often happen to people who break easily, or have sharp edges, or who have to be carefully kept. Generally, by the time you are Real, most of your hair has been loved off, and your eyes drop out and you get loose in the joints and very shabby. But these things don't matter at all, because once you are Real you can't be ugly, except to people who don't understand."

—Margery Williams, *The Velveteen Rabbit*

Objects of Desire

BREWED WITH PURE MOUNTAIN SPRING WATER

Whirlaway   *Sea-Biscuit*   *Man O' War*

Rolling Rock Beer

LATROBE BREWING COMPANY, LATROBE, PENNSYLV...

202
Rolling Rock beer
advertisements

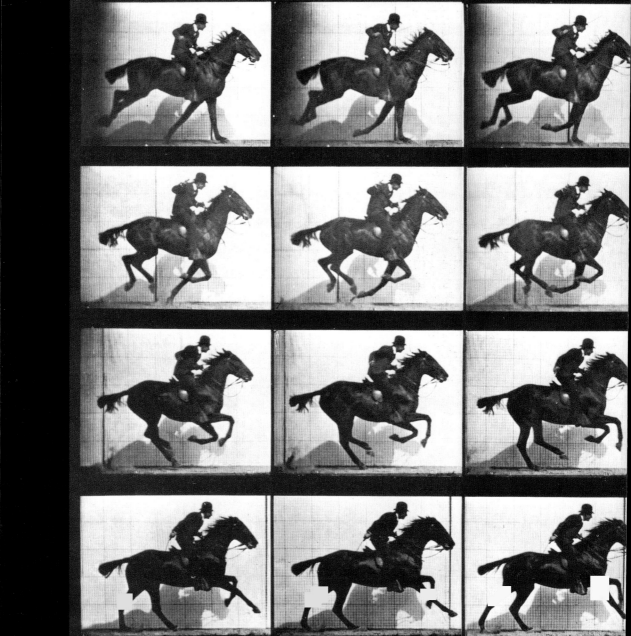

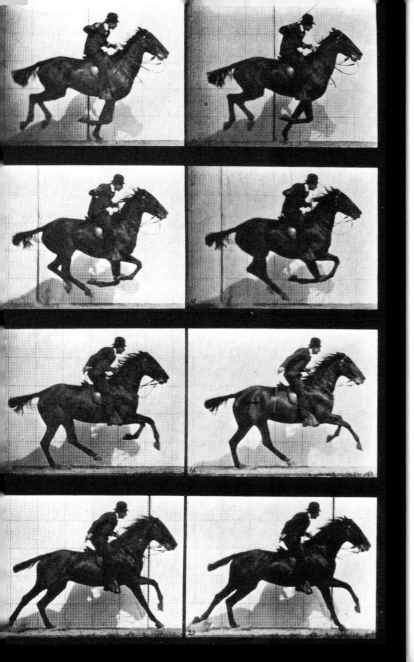

Eadweard Muybridge photographs

In 1877, wealthy California racehorse breeder Leland Stanford asked photographer Eadweard Muybridge to help him settle a bet; Stanford believed that all four of a running horse's legs are off the ground at the same time. With a primitive strobe light, Muybridge made the first stop-action photos, of Stanford's horse Occident, proving Stanford right. Muybridge went on to make many other motion studies and invented a device for viewing them, the zoopraxiscope, that earned him credit as the inventor of the first motion pictures.

239
Favorite recordings of horse songs

"Camptown Races"
Written by Stephen Foster in the mid-1800s, "Camptown Races" celebrates the famous Flora Temple, a bob-tailed trotter.

"Stewball"
In the late 1700s a race took place near Dublin between a skewbald horse owned by Sir Arthur Marvel and a gray mare named Miss Portly, owned by Sir Ralph Gore.

Kenny Loggins, "All the Pretty Little Ponies"

Jethro Tull, "Heavy Horses"

K. D. Lang, "Pullin' Back the Reins"

Dan Fogelberg, "Run for the Roses"

Michael Murphy, "Wildfire"

"A Horse Is a Horse," the Mr. Ed theme song

"The Old Gray Mare," folk song

The Byrds, "The Chestnut Mare"

"Old Paint," folk song

Lyle Lovitt, "If I Had a Boat"

Emmy Lou Harris, "The Sweetheart of the Rodeo"

Patsy Montana, "I Want to Be a Cowboy's Sweetheart"

Michael Murphy, "Ponies"

Johnny Cash, "The Tennessee Stud"

Richard Thompson, "The Angels Have Taken My Racehorse Away"

240
Gene Autry,
the singing
cowboy

GLOBE
TROTTING

EQUESTRIAN ADVENTURES

Even if you never ride a horse beyond your own backyard, it's fun to imagine the limitless possibilities, if money were no object and youth and horsemanship were on your side.

241 Riding white Andalusians on the white beaches of Andalusia

The powerful, elegant Andalusian horse of the Iberian Peninsula became the "royal horse of Europe" and the foundation breed of the famed Lipizzaners.

242 Attending the swimming of the ponies at Chincoteague

Since 1925, on the last Wednesday of every July, the wild ponies that live on Assateague Island, off the coast of Maryland, have been rounded up and herded across the Chincoteague Bay to Chincoteague. Approximately seventy foals and yearlings are auctioned off each year on the following day, to keep the size of the wild population stable.

243 Pony trekking in Wales

Complete with picnics and camping, pony trekking is a popular pastime in Wales.

244 The looking-glass perfection of the Lipizzaners' quadrille

This amazing display of horsemanship is made more spectacular by its setting: the splendid Baroque architecture of the Spanish Riding School in Vienna.

245 Flying to Reykjavík to experience the *tölt*
of the Icelandic horse

The small, sturdy Icelandic horse has a unique gait called
the *tölt*, an extremely smooth four-beat running walk that
allows the rider a virtually bounce-free ride at speeds up to
20 miles per hour, excellent for trail-riding or trekking.

246 Covering your eyes as the horses take on
Becher's Brook in the Grand National

A unique test of horse and horsemanship, the Grand
National, held every year at Aintree Racecourse in
Liverpool, England, is the most famous steeplechase in
the world. During the first race, in 1839, Captain Martin
Becher fell from his horse Conrad into the brook when in
the lead. To this day, the sixth jump on the first circuit,
which stands six feet nine inches high on the far side due
to a two-foot drop, remains one of the most formidable
fences of the race.

247 Jousting tournaments in Maryland

In 1962 the Maryland General Assembly made jousting
the official sport of Maryland; its proponents pointed to
jousting's links to ancient traditions of chivalry. It
remained the state sport until 2004, when it was
replaced by lacrosse.

248 Trail-riding along the beaches of Invercargill, New
Zealand, with Stewart Island as a backdrop

249
Adopting a wild horse

In 1971, because large herds of wild horses and burros were competing for grass with domestic livestock and also causing soil erosion, the federal government established the Wild Horse and Burro Adoption Program. Unbranded, unclaimed, and free-roaming horses and burros are rounded up and offered for adoption at locations across the country.

252 Eating great Tex-Mex at the Fort Worth Stock Show and Rodeo

253 Sipping a chilled zinfandel on the sidelines of the polo field in Portsmith, Rhode Island

254 Bringing home an Irish draught horse from the Irish Horse Fair in Ballinasloe, Ireland

255 Hearing the gong and the roll of the drums when your polo team scores in Japan

256 Riding a well-trained trail horse through the Monteverde Cloud Forest in Costa Rica

250 Rubbing elbows with the racing elite at the Fasig-Tipton yearling sales in Saratoga, New York
The crème de la crème of racing pedigrees, horses are led into the arena by handlers in tuxedoes, the auctioneer croons, and buyers raise a finger or an eyebrow as the digitally lit price climbs to astronomical heights.

251 Attending the Kentucky Rolex Three-Day Event at the Kentucky Horse Park in Lexington

257 Drinking champagne and watching *grand prix* jumping at Madison Square Garden

258 Riding in the sulky simulator at the Harness Racing Museum & Hall of Fame in Goshen, New York

259 Going to the Belmont Stakes to see if this is the year for the Triple Crown

260 Riding once around Central Park in New York City

261 Riding domesticated Camargue ponies through flamingo breeding grounds in southeastern France

The original wild ponies, which have coexisted with the wildlife of the region since prehistoric times, run through the marshlands in a triangle of land called the Camargue.

262 Watching your horse win on the world's largest TV in Hong Kong

The infield of the Sha Tin racecourse holds the Guinness world record for a television screen: 26 by 230 feet.

263 Sleeping in a yurt with your Mongolian horse tethered outside the door

The true wild Mongolian horse, Przewalski's horse, is being reintroduced to Mongolia and China after nearing extinction.

264 Experiencing the pampas with gauchos from the back of a Criollo

The Criollo is a working horse used to herd cattle. It is also the star of Argentina's national sport, polo, and serves as the symbol of Latin American horse culture.

265 Drinking fermented mare's milk at the Litang Festival, in Tibet

Each year during the first week of August over two thousand horsemen gather with family and friends on the high grassland plateau to compete in a series of events. The acrobatic competition shows off the extraordinary riding skills of the Litang horsemen, who ride standing up in the saddle or hanging from their horse's underbelly, or swoop down to scoop up articles on the ground, while galloping on mounts bedecked with bronze bells, scarlet blankets, and embroidered saddles and bridles. Other events include long-distance racing, endurance trekking, horse trading, singing, dancing, and feasting.

270
Examining the horses at
the Draft Horse Sale in
Kalona, Iowa

Destrier is the medieval term for a
war horse. In tournaments the
horses wore flowing
caparisons, or capes,
stenciled with symbols
from the knight's coat
of arms.

276
Seeing the ponies of Ocracoke Island

Ocracoke Island, on the Outer Banks of North Carolina, was once the pastureland of a group of feral ponies believed to descend from horses that escaped from foundered Spanish ships in the 1500s. In the 1950s, retired Major Marvin Howard founded the mounted Boy Scout Troop 209. Members of the troop picked out a wild horse, trained it, rode it, then released it back to the wild. Every year the troop would also compete in the annual race at Buxton. Each scout would catch his pony, ride it the seventeen miles to the ferry, hold the pony on the open deck during the crossing, and then ride to Buxton for the race. Ocracoke ponies were known to beat stiff competition from Arabians and quarter horses, even after their twenty-six-mile ride. In the 1960s, the Boy Scouts of America demanded that insurance be purchased if the troop was to continue to ride horses. Since the troop did not have the funds to cover the insurance, the glorious decade of mounted Troop 209 came to an end.

277
Dining at The Noble Horse in Chicago

An 1877 livery stable in Chicago's Old Town houses The Noble Horse Dinner Theatre, as well as the city's carriage horses. The theater serves dinner complete with an equestrian performance. Jumping exhibitions, the quadrille, and vaulting are on the menu for a unique evening!

278
Being sprayed by ice and snow as the horses make the turn at the St. Moritz horse races

The "white turf" held each winter in St Moritz is an event of skill and daring drawing an international crowd of spectators, as well as reknowned horse owners and jockeys. In one of the world's most beautiful settings, horse races are held on a frozen lake with one unique event, "skikjöring"—riderless horses galloping at full speed pulling daredevil skiers around the course.

279

Volunteering to be on the horse committee at the nearest hippotherapy facility

Hippotherapy, a form of treatment using horses, derives its name from the Greek word for horse, *hippos*. Children and adults with varying disabilities benefit from the swinging stride of the horse—a movement that can increase muscle tone, relax otherwise spastic muscles, and improve posture and motor skill—motivating them to extend themselves beyond their usual mobility.

Hippotherapy, or therapeutic riding centers, exist in almost every state in the United States, but it is still not covered here by health insurance, as the therapy is in Europe. As a result, most therapeutic riding centers depend heavily on volunteers. This can be logistically difficult to arrange, since for each rider there must be a team consisting of an instructor and/or physical therapist, a horse handler, and one or two "sidewalkers", as well as a group to care for and prepare the horse. The rewards gained by the participants, both riders and volunteers, are tremendous.

280
Touring the historic
horse country of Kentucky

289
Watching mustangs roam
the endless prairie at
The Black Hills Wild Horse
Sanctuary outside
Hot Springs, South Dakota

Taking your horse to a clinic with Monty Roberts, Buck Brannaman, John Lyons, or Pat Parelli

The term *horse whisperer* has been with us since ancient times, when the horse was essential in everyday life, and miracle cures for misunderstood and mistreated horses were greatly in demand. Some successful "horse whisperers" were burned at the stake as witches, while others were mere charlatans using brute force behind closed doors.

Today the horse whisperer has resurfaced, popularized by movies and literature. Many modern trainers, whether they embrace the term or vehemently resist it, have adopted a similar technique. They are actually listening to the horse, rather than whispering to it. Rather than "breaking" a horse, they find it not only more humane but also more successful to "gentle" it. Haltering and leading is introduced by using the natural instinct of the foal to follow its dam. When the colt or filly is ready for more advanced training, the principles of herd behavior are used to establish dominance in a round pen, followed by extensive groundwork. Finally the horse is ridden and learns to respond to riding aids through gentle pressure-and-release techniques that reward the horse for desired behavior. The riding aids themselves are based on horses' natural instincts.

It has always been true that some people have a remarkable gift for working with animals, due to their demeanor, confidence, and skills. "Horse whispering" conveys just the quiet, gentle patience these personalities embody.

291
Standing in the sunlight of the Palazzo Publico in Siena on the day of the Palio

The Palio race, held each August, is a battle of politics, religion, and neighborhood pride. The neighborhoods, or *contradas*, whose origins date back to the military division of Siena, Italy in the Middle Ages, conduct a fierce rivalry that is most evident during the Palio.

The ritual begins in late April, with colorful processions honoring the patron saint of each neighborhood, followed by the *trattative*, or negotiation, where the horses are assigned by lot, the jockeys are named, and the plotting and treachery begin. Thousands of dollars move from one *contrada* to another as myriad schemes are hatched; as a result, both jockeys and horses are heavily guarded from the day of the *trattative* until the main race. Six trial races are run so that riders can become accustomed to their mounts.

On the eve of the Palio, a huge feast is held in the Palazzo Publico. Tables laden with various dishes are set up around the square. Throughout the feast conversation centers on the merits of each *contrada*, the skill of the riders, and rumors of secret alliances. The next morning, the horses are led into their neighborhood church, where the priest blesses them.

On race day, three hours of pageantry entertain the cheering crowd. Finally, two white bulls enter the square carrying the *palio*, or banner. The horses and riders take their places behind a rope held up as a starting gate; upon its release, jockeys fearlessly maneuver their thundering mounts three times around the Palazzo in a frenzied free-for-all. A breathtaking 90 seconds later, the race is over. The *palio* is then presented to the captain of the winning *contrada*, and immediately afterward, fans follow the winning jockey and horse to their neighborhood church to thank God for their victory.

292
The Harness Racing Museum
and Hall of Fame,
Goshen, New York

Horse Museums

HISTORIC TRACK
"CRADLE OF THE TROTTER"
MADE FAMOUS BY
HAMBLETONIAN (1849-1876)
SIRE OF TROTTERS
STATE EDUCATION
DEPARTMENT 1950

THE QUEST FOR EXCELLENCE

The Spirit of the American West

The wild horse is the symbol of the American West but in reality it is the domesticated horse that provided the American Indian and settler with the ability to transport, hunt large game, and ranch. Some horses still work on ranches, others learn the trade for showmanship. The Western horse is honored for its adaptability, versatility, strength, agility and companionship in a variety of tests of skill provided in rodeos and Western horse shows across the nation.

THE RODEO

309 Cheyenne Frontier Days
Four parades, three pancake breakfasts, forty bull rides, twenty-eight bareback rides, and wild-horse racing—fun-filled family entertainment each July in Cheyenne, Wyoming.

310 The Salinas Rodeo
Marketed as "the original extreme sport," the Salinas Rodeo in Salinas, California, has honored the life of the cowboy since 1911.

311 The Wrangler National Rodeo Finals
The fifteen top Aussie rodeo stars from the National Pro Tour series compete in roughriding and timed events. Held in Toowoomba, Queensland, Australia, first week in December.

312 The Calgary Stampede
The world's top cowboys have been competing for supremacy since 1912 at this event in Calgary, Alberta, Canada, billed as "The Greatest Outdoor Show on Earth."

Cowboy Luke Walker is ejected from a horse called Rock N Roll in the Bareback Bronc Riding event at the Calgary Stampede, 2004

313
The excitement of the Pendleton Round-Up

In 1909 Pendleton, Oregon, held a Fourth of July celebration, with greased-pig races, bronc riding, horse racing between Indians and non-Indians, Indian feasts, and war dances. It was such a success that the community made it an annual event known as the Pendleton Round-Up. The celebration was moved to September so local farmers could attend after the harvest.

The Pendleton Round-Up is now one of the premier rodeo venues in the United States, celebrating both cowboy and American Indian heritage. Surviving burned grandstands and horse barns, murders and fatal accidents, wars and the Great Depression, the spirit of the American West prevails.

Prairie Rose Henderson, early 1900s champion bronc rider. The crowds loved her homemade costumes of feathers, fringe and beads.

314
That giddy-up feeling of western wear

"Cow Girls" at the PENDLETON "ROUND UP" 1911

Rodeo Queens

The first rodeo queen on record was Bertha Anger, crowned at the 1910 Pendleton Round-Up for selling the most tickets to the event. In years to follow the title of Rodeo Queen at Pendleton was dominated by the daughters and fiancées of prominent cattlemen and horsemen. In 1918 the title was terminated with an announcement in the *East Oregonian* that "the rodeo would return as an institution of the common people."

The reign of rodeo queens began again at Pendleton in 1921 and is today a staple of county fairs across the nation. To prepare for rodeo pageants, the Queen Camp in Kelleyville, Oklahoma, now serves as a finishing school where contestants can hone their horsewomanship skills as well as their royal manners. The Miss Rodeo America Pageant is held in Las Vegas each December in conjunction with the National Finals Rodeo.

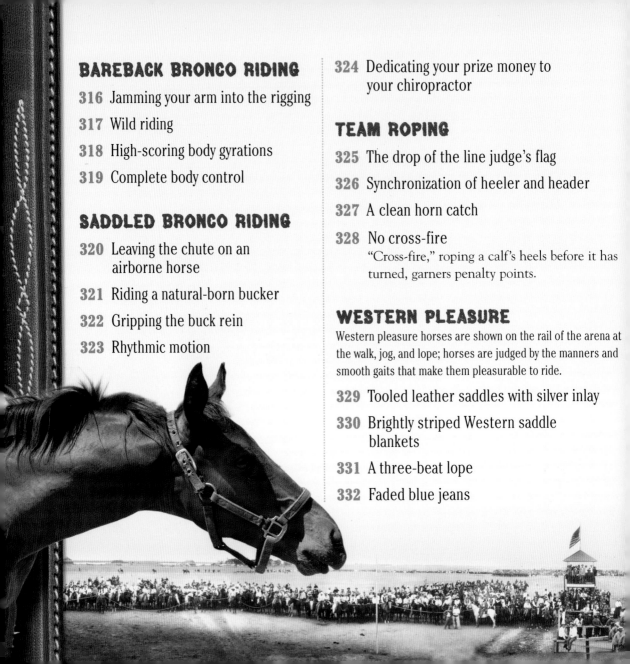

REINING

Horse and rider maneuver through a set pattern, demonstrating the horse's ability to change leads, turn, and stop.

LUCILLE MULHALL WORLD'S CHAMPION LADY

CALF ROPING

TEER ROPER "STAMPEDE" WINNIPEG 1913

BARREL RACING

Horse and rider circle three barrels in a cloverleaf pattern before leaving the ring, racing against the clock.

358 Exploding into the arena

359 Competing against the clock

360 Running so fast they don't know what you're wearing

361 Fast-paced cloverleaves

362 Riding a deep-seated saddle

363 Ripping through the course

364 Leaving the arena with all three up

CUTTING

Cutting demonstrates a horse and rider's ability to control a cow as effortlessly as possible.

365 Just you, the cow, and the horse

366 Allowing no daylight between you and your horse

367 A horse that can stop, turn, rate, and read cattle

368 A trained and responsive mount

369 Maneuvering a cow away from the herd

370 Turning the job over to your horse

371 Dropping the reins

372 Gripping the saddle horn

373 A nose-to-nose standoff

374 The ride of your life

TEAM PENNING

A team of three horses and three riders works against the clock to separate three cows from the herd and place them in a pen at the end of the arena.

375 Memorizing the cows' numbers

376 Entering the herd

377 Relying on your turnback to hold dirty cows

378 Studying the cow's ear communication

379 Pushing a cow down the fence

380 Making a great new friend in a randomly chosen "draw-pot" team

381 The exhilaration of teamwork

382 Reevaluating each turn with your teammates over a cold beer

spoke

honda

loop

chaps

lasso

FLORENCE LA DUE,

WORLD'S CHAMPION LADY FANCY ROPE

SPINNING 75 FEET OF ROPE,

The flat loop

The language of the rodeo

The language of the rodeo has always reflected the Spanish heritage and tradition of the Southwest and neighboring Mexico. Rodeo comes from **RODEAR**, the verb meaning "to go around," which itself, interestingly enough, derives from the old Spanish **RODE**, a horse ring. Lasso is the Spanish **LAZO**, while lariat includes the article with the noun for "rope" or "thong," **LA REATA**. Mustang comes from **MESTENO**, a half-breed horse, while bronco takes the adjective from **POTRO BRONCO**, wild colt. Chaps is merely a shortened form of the name in Spanish, **CHAPARAJOS**.

—Luigi Gianoli,
*Horses and Horsemanship
through the Ages*

EG "STAMPEDE" 1913,

THE REFINEMENT OF ENGLISH HORSEMANSHIP

What we today refer to as English equitation is actually based on the traditions of various European schools of riding. Western riding traditions evolved from the horsemanship of ranch work. English traditions evolved from horsemanship for pleasure and sport.

From the days of nobility to the present time, the desire to show your horse in all its grandeur, with elegance and style, survives. Steeped in a tradition of refined schooling and dress, the various English disciplines display the eloquent athleticism of the horse.

Britain's Princess Elizabeth, later Queen Elizabeth II, at a horse show in 1934

English Pleasure

Judged on the true pleasure quality and performance of the horse, and the neatness and appearance of both horse and rider.

385 Round, fluid front-end motion

386 Proper manners from both you and your horse

387 A horse that's light in the bridle, with a quiet mouth

388 Demonstrating balance within the frame

389 Bridle rosettes

390 Comfortable field boots

391 Bringing out a bloom on your horse's coat

392 Elegant black tack on a dark bay

393 The rhythm of a collected canter

394 Pride in a bold and commanding performance

395 Soft applause as you line up for judging

Eventing or Combined Training

An event or combined training horse trial takes place over one to three days, during which horse and rider are tested in dressage, show jumping, and cross-country jumping.

408
Summoning courage
to match that of a
fearless horse

Poltroon

409
Poltroon
"The Little Horse That Could," this 15.1-hand charismatic paint mare won the bronze in combined training at the Alternate Olympic Games, 1980, ridden by Torrance Watkins.

410
Primmore's Pride
Pippa Funnell's mount in two of the three legs of eventing's Grand Slam, Burghley and Badminton, both in England. Funnell, who is the first rider to claim this prize since it was offered in 1998, won the other leg, the Rolex Kentucky in Lexington, Kentucky, on another horse, Supreme Rock.

411
Custom Made
A 17.2-hand dark bay Irish Thoroughbred, Custom Made carried David O'Connor to America's first Olympic gold in eventing, at the 2000 Sydney Olympics.

Dressage

Dressage, in French, means simply "training," but it could also be described as ballet for horse and rider. The discipline of dressage seeks to enhance the natural movement of the horse through a subtle, harmonious use of the rider's body language and a careful system of athletic conditioning, and judges these qualities in the performance of set patterns of movements.

413 Scoring a "10" in walk

414 Collection

415 Keeping your horse round

416 Wearing a top hat and tails

417 Floating on a half-pass

418 Getting excited over "lipstick"

Foam around a horse's mouth—called "lipstick"—is highly prized as a sign that the horse is mouthing the bit in a soft, relaxed way.

419 Laughing about "dressage queens" —even if you are one!

420 Moving up to a double bridle

421 A swallowtail saddle pad with gold trim

422 Full-seat breeches

423 Warming up at the schooling ring at Devon

Dressage at Devon, held in late September and early October in Devon, Pennsylvania, combines a world-class dressage competition and the world's largest open breed show with an international fall festival.

424 Finally earning your scores for your USDF medal

425 The exquisite control of piaffe and passage

Passage is a suspended, elevated trot with a pause at the high point of each stride; piaffe, a trot on one spot, requires supreme balance and strength, and is considered the ultimate in collection.

426 Waiting to get your test back from the scribe

427 Knowing you look good in black and white

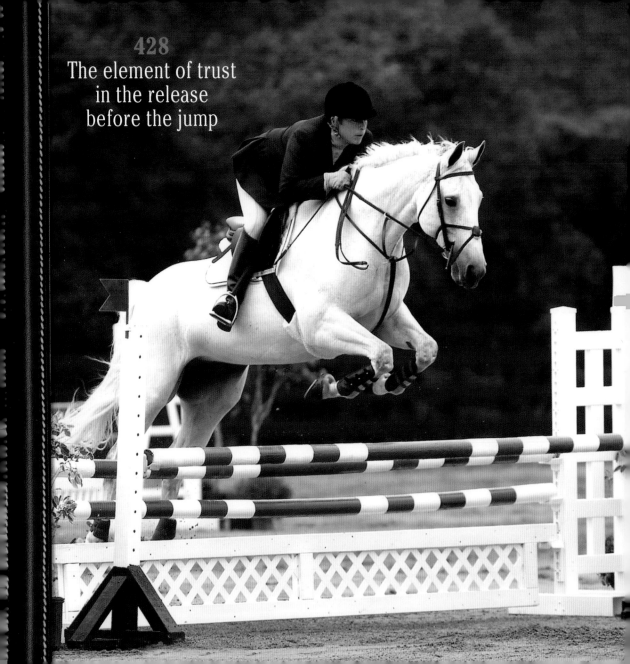

The element of trust
in the release
before the jump

Show Jumping

Show or stadium jumping is a sport based on penalties and faults in jumping a course of various types of obstacles; unlike jumping in hunter classes, it is based entirely on the ability of the horse to jump fast and clear, not on style.

429 The Caprilli seat

Federico Caprilli, an Italian cavalry officer, in the late 1800s revolutionized the world of equitation with his novel forward jumping seat, in which the rider crouches in balance over the stirrups, staying up and out of the saddle, instead of leaning back and shoving his legs forward, the accepted style of the time.

430 Figure-eight nosebands

431 Because you always wanted to wear a scarlet coat

432 The most exciting forty seconds of your life

433 Riding the bounce

434 Not having to worry about "style points"

435 In tack, anything goes

436 Fleece-lined open-front jumping boots

437 A horse born to jump water obstacles

438 Checkering on your horse's hindquarters

Patterns such as checkers and diamonds, made by brushing against the lay of the horse's hair, highlight the conformation of the hindquarters and show off a clean, glossy coat.

439 Liverpool jumps

440 Garish oxers

441 Navigating the pillared jumps at the Hampton Classic

The Hampton Classic Horse Show, held over the Labor Day weekend in Bridgehampton, New York, is the largest hunter-jumper show in the United States.

442 Making the jump-off

443 Big Ben

This 17.3-hand chestnut Belgian warmblood, ridden by the Canadian Ian Millar, won more than forty Grand Prix titles, including six Spruce Meadow Derbies and two consecutive World Cup Championships (1987 and 1988).

Saddle-Seat Equitation

An elegant, stylish form of riding, uniquely American, developed in the colonial era to show off the high neck carriage and flamboyant gaits of certain breeds of horses.

444 Entering the ring with style and attitude

445 Picture-perfect posture in a Lane Fox saddle

446 A well-dressed park horse in a Weymouth bridle

The Weymouth, or double, bridle uses two bits and two sets of reins, offering finer control. The snaffle (or bradoon) bit acts to raise the horse's head, while the curb bit helps to flex it.

447 An elegant dark saddle suit with a matching bowler

448 Jodhpur boots spotless from top to sole

Judges have been known to check the soles of contestants' boots for cleanliness.

449 Looking poised in a ground-covering, smooth walk on a National Show Horse

The National Show Horse blends the characteristics of the Arabian and the American saddlebred to create a horse that combines elegance with athleticism and stamina; to be registered, a foal must have at least 25 percent and no more than 99 percent Arabian blood.

450 The fast, flashy rack of the American saddlebred

451 A chic, high-headed, neatly clipped horse

452 The imperceptible movements of gloved hands

453 The elegance of riding in a tuxedo after six o'clock

Hunters

Hunters are judged on conformation, suitability, manners, quality of movement, and responsiveness to the rider's cues; over fences, the jumping style of both horse and rider is as important as whether the horse clears the fence.

462
Horse-show
memories
preserved in a
scrapbook

SUSSEX

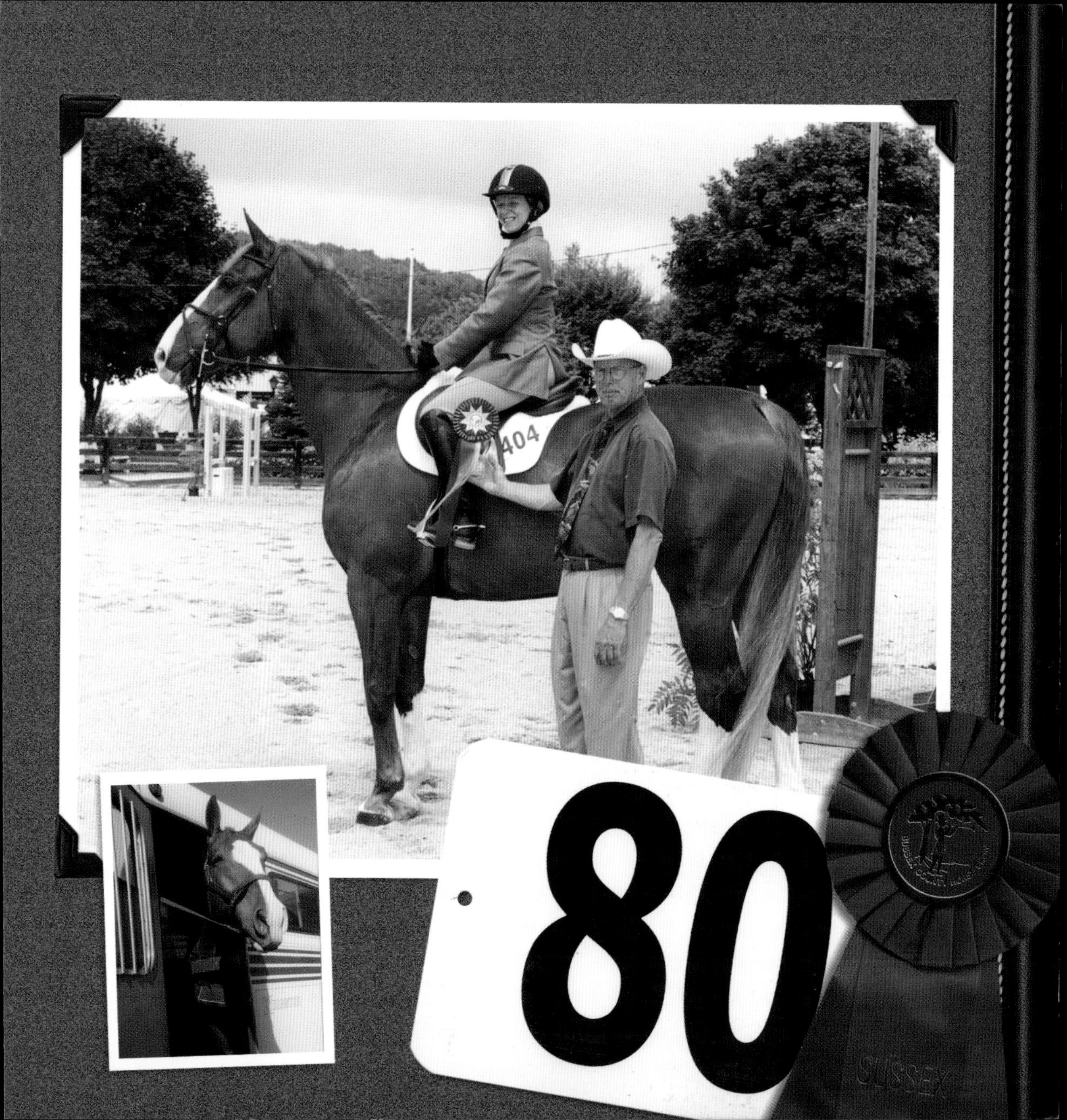

404
80
SUSSEX

Foxhunting

Historically a sport of the upper classes, fox-hunting originated in the effort of landowners to rid their land of vermin. In England and Wales, foxhunting was banned in 2004.

463 The mist rising off the grass

464 The sound of the copper horn

465 A powerful draft-cross mount

466 Hounds giving tongue

467 Velvety hunt caps

468 Stock ties

469 Picking up the scent

470 The red of the hunt master's coat

471 The prestige of mahogany- cuffed boots

472 Sailing over a rocky outcrop

473 Tipping your hat to the master of the foxhounds

474 The whipper-in's call of "Hark, halloa"

475 The thrill of the cry "Forrand away!"

476 Hunting with the Myopia Hunt Club
The original five members of this club in Hamilton, Massachusetts, the oldest and most prestigious hunt club in America, all wore glasses.

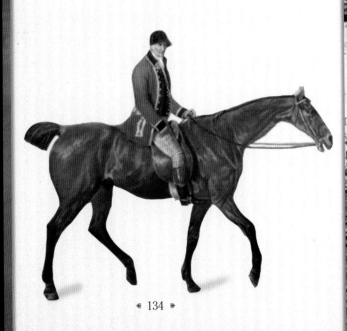

Polo

The Federation of International Polo stages a championship event every three years in a different host country. Brazil was the 2003 champion.

Vaulting

Gymnastics performed on the back of a horse.

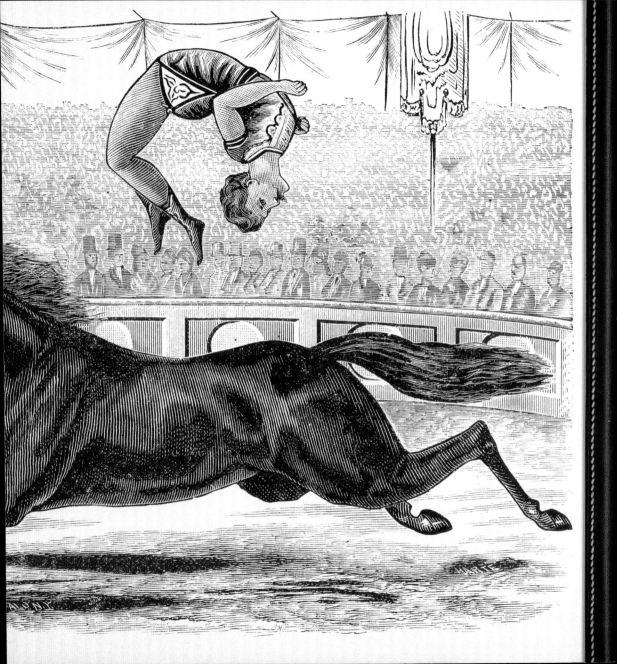

A Shared Passion

Horses like to gather in herds; to some extent, so do people. The pleasure of horse-related activities only increases in a group, and who can tell whether the horse, the rider, or the community at large benefits most?

498 The Texas Ladies Aside

The Texas Ladies Aside is a Paso Fino sidesaddle drill team made up of women ages fifteen to sixty-five. They perform in flamboyant costume in parades and exhibitions across the nation, sharing camaraderie, the love of the Paso Fino, a Peruvian breed of horse with a flashy but very comfortable gait, and the pride of representing the state of Texas. They have recently been honored with the designation Official Equestrian Drill Team of Texas.

499 The American Cream Draft Horse Association

An organization to develop and improve the American Cream Draft, the only draft horse breed to have originated in the United States.

500 El Capa Bareback Riders

A group of forty to fifty motivated young riders ages eight to nineteen who ride and perform bareback, without bridles, even jumping sixteen abreast.

The Round Up B

501 The Nez Percé Appaloosa Horse Club
An organization formed to help reintroduce the Appaloosa horse to the Nez Percé Indian Reservation.

502 The Old People's Riding Club
A group dedicated to providing for adults the education youngsters gain in Pony Club.

503 The Medieval Horse Guild
Guild members learn about horsemanship techniques from the Middle Ages and engage in "horse wars," games, and parades in medieval costume.

504 The Santa Fe County Sheriff's Posse
Posse volunteers train for and conduct horseback search-and-rescue operations.

505 The Mounted Band of the Royal Lifeguards
Move to Stockholm, Sweden, and ride a Shire (a gift from the Queen of England) or a Swedish Thoroughbred in parades while playing trumpets, tubas, and kettle drums.

506 The Honolulu Polo Club
"E noho'ana Polo" means "Celebrate the polo lifestyle." These people—with cocktails, leis, glowing tans, and Hawaiian shirts—seem to be having serious fun.

507 The Horselover's Connection
A dating service that helps you find that perfect cowboy or gal.

508 The Yodeladies
Founded by coauthors Sheri Seggerman and Mary Tiegreen, the Yodeladies are dedicated to promoting kindness to horses.

"Pendleton Ore 1911"

ICONIC HORSES & RIDERS

The image of the horse often translates into the symbol of the horse—courageous, invincible, wise. Horses both mythical and historical have become symbols, and often their riders share in the glory.

509 The centaur
This creature of Greek mythology, half human, half horse, represents the struggle between good and evil, god and beast.

510 Bucephalus
Alexander the Great won this fiery mount as a boy of twelve when, realizing that the horse was fearful of his own shadow, he was able to ride him by facing him toward the sun.

511 Sleipnir
The magical eight-legged steed of the Norse god Odin, Sleipnir conveys Odin between the realms of spirit and matter and is symbolic of Time.

512 Epona
The Celtic goddess Epona, protectress of horses, animals, riders, and stables, is most often portrayed riding a horse or feeding foals from a basket of fruits and grains. Many ancient stables kept a shrine to Epona. On the day of the Feast of Epona, grooms would decorate this shrine with the goddess's flower, the rose, and all the working animals would get a holiday.

513 The Trojan Horse
In Homer's *Iliad*, the Greeks make a gift to the Trojans of a large wooden horse; the horse, which concealed soldiers, was actually a ruse to penetrate the walls of Troy and destroy it.

514
Pegasus

This mythological horse carried thunderbolts for Zeus, was ridden by Eos each morning to pull in the dawn, created the Fountain of Hippocrene from which flows inspiration for poets, and is credited with making the sound effect we call thunder by galloping across the sky during a storm.

What's the use of
having magic,
if you can't save
a unicorn?

—Peter S. Beagle,
The Last Unicorn

515 The unicorn

Rarely seen, the unicorn remains in hiding due to the never-ending quest of hunters to obtain its single horn, which is endowed with magical powers. The unicorn will only show itself to people of unquestionable virtue.

516 Lady Godiva

A horsewoman true to her convictions, on a challenge from her husband Lady Godiva rode in the nude through the streets of Coventry, England, to persuade him to lower the taxes on peasants.

517 Tziman Chac, Cortés, and the Itza

On leaving the Yucatán Peninsula, the conquistador Hernan Cortés left a lame horse with the Itza, a Mayan tribe, saying he would retrieve it when he returned. Having never seen a horse, the Itza treated it like a god and fed it fowl and meat. Not surprisingly, the horse died, and the people built a large idol of a horse in its honor, calling it Tziman Chac, "Thunder Horse."

518 Marco Polo

The Italian explorer Marco Polo rode on horseback across the Far East in A.D. 1300, keeping extensive notes on the varieties of horses and horsemanship he encountered.

519 Incitatus

The mad Roman emperor Caligula had a favorite horse, Incitatus, who drank from golden troughs, wore jeweled collars, and dined with heads of state at the table while much of the populace starved. Just prior to his assassination, Caligula made Incitatus a senator.

520 The Uffington White Horse

The purpose and origin of the Uffington Horse, the largest of the horse figures carved into chalky hills in England, remain unknown. Dated to the Bronze Age, the horse may have been made by worshipers of Epona, the horse goddess, or Belinos, the sun god, who was also associated with horses. In all, there are twenty-four hillside horses in Britain, the majority carved in the last three hundred years.

521 Shadowfax

Chief of the Mearas, lords of horses, Shadowfax was Gandalf's steed in *The Lord of the Rings*.

522 Rocinante

In Miguel de Cervantes's novel *Don Quixote*, the would-be knight borrows his neighbor's worn-out old horse as his charger. *Rocinante* means "super-nag," and this horse is trustworthy and faithful throughout Don Quixote's misadventures.

The Cherhill Horse, England,
carved in 1780

523 The dancing white horse and Sitting Bull

For a period of time, Sitting Bull performed on a white horse in Buffalo Bill Cody's Wild West Show. When Sitting Bull left, Buffalo Bill gave him the horse as a gift. Later, during a battle that would end Sitting Bull's life, the white horse, trained to dance at the sound of gunfire, performed his entire routine of dancing, circling, rearing, and bowing. Lakota legend states that the white horse danced in the chief's honor.

524 Nelson and George Washington

Due to his calmness under fire, Nelson was Washington's favorite mount.

525 Little Sorrel and Stonewall Jackson

The favorite mount of Jackson, Little Sorrel was stuffed after his death and is now on display at the Virginia Military Institute Museum.

526 Copenhagen and Wellington

Wellington rode Copenhagen—of whom he said, "there may have been many faster horses, no doubt many handsomer, but for bottom and endurance I never saw his fellow"—in the Battle of Waterloo.

527 Black Jack

Named after General Pershing, Black Jack was the last horse to be commissioned by the quartermaster to the U.S. Army, and the last horse to carry the "U.S." brand. He functioned as the riderless horse, carrying reversed black boots in his stirrups in thousands of funeral processions at Arlington, including those of presidents Herbert Hoover, John F. Kennedy, Lyndon B. Johnson, and General Douglas MacArthur.

Black Jack, the riderless horse, at the funeral of John F. Kennedy

COMANCHE THE ONLY SURVIVOR OF THE CUSTER MASSACRE 1876. HISTORY OF THE HORSE AND REGIMENTAL ORDERS OF THE 7TH CAVALRY AS TO THE CARE OF "COMANCHE" AS LONG AS HE SHALL LIVE PHOTOGRAPHED AND COPYRIGHTED BY J.C. H... ... ...STURGIS D... 1887.

528 Marengo and Napoleon

Napoleon's most famous horse, Marengo, his steed in the Battle of Waterloo, was later captured by the British.

529 Comanche

This fifteen-hand bay mustang-cross gelding, Captain Myles Keogh's mount, was the only U.S. Cavalry survivor of the Battle of Little Big Horn.

530
Traveller and Robert E. Lee

Robert E. Lee's mount through most of the Civil War outlived the General and was buried at the Lee Chapel.

Traveller

WHEN MARKIE LEE ASKED TO PAINT TRAVELLER'S PORTRAIT,
GENERAL LEE REPLIED:

If I was an artist like you, I would draw a true picture of Traveller; representing his fine proportions, muscular figure, deep chest, short back, strong haunches, flat legs, small head, broad forehead, delicate ears, quick eye, small feet, and black mane and tail. Such a picture would inspire a poet, whose genius could then depict his worth, and describe his endurance of toil, hunger, thirst, heat and cold; and the dangers and suffering through which he has passed. He could dilate upon his sagacity and affection, and his invariable response to every wish of his rider. He might even imagine his thoughts through the long night-marches and days of the battle through which he has passed. But I am no artist Markie, and can therefore only say he is a Confederate grey.

—Robert E. Lee

531
Horse wisdom
Many common adages date back to the era of the horse.

Don't put the cart before the horse.

The pace makes the race.

It's no use closing the stable door after the horse has gone.

You can lead a horse to water, but you can't make it drink.

Don't look a gift horse in the mouth.

If wishes were horses, beggars would ride.

Different courses for different horses.

Breed to the best and hope for the best.

No hoof, no horse.

532
Locating the constellation Pegasus
in the night sky

533
Pretending your horse has wings

534
Imagining yourself as Lady Godiva

535
Realizing that even Bellerophon
got bucked off Pegasus when the
horse was bitten by a gadfly

536
Dressing your horse in medieval
armor for the Renaissance Fair

537
Dreaming of how your horse
would look hitched to a
golden two-horse chariot

538
The Horsehead Nebula

First discovered in the late 1800s, the
Horsehead Nebula is located approximately
1,500 light years from Earth in the constellation
of Orion. Also known as Barnard 33, it is
composed of thick dust and gases silhouetted
against the bright emission nebula, IC 434.

539
Monty Roberts

Author of the 1997 *New York Times* bestseller *The Man Who Listens to Horses*, Roberts popularized a form of gentle horse training based on the horse's natural body language.

MODERN HEROES

540 Dayton O. Hyde

A conservationist, Dayton O. Hyde established the Institute of the Range and American Mustang (IRAM), a nonprofit organization that provides a better quality of life for America's wild horses. The organization's Black Hills Wild Horse Sanctuary resettles unwanted mustangs on 11,000 acres in South Dakota. The sanctuary supports itself through private donation, tourism, gift shops, and the sale of foals.

541 Colonel Alois Podhajsky

In 1945 Podhajsky, the head of the Spanish Riding School in Vienna, negotiated the evacuation of the school's Lipizzan stallions prior to the Russian invasion, and later convinced General Patton to rescue the Lipizzan mares as part of the Allied prisoner liberation program. Podhajsky wrote a number of classic texts on horsemanship, among them his memoir *My Horses, My Teachers*.

542 Kim Zito

With her husband, trainer Nick Zito, she has worked to raise public awareness of the need for thoroughbred retirement, adopted horses in need, and helped with the establishment and support of several horse retirement and rescue foundations.

543 Laura Hillenbrandt

Hillenbrandt's bestselling 2001 book, *Seabiscuit* (later to become a movie), boosted attendance records at racetracks across the nation.

544 Bo Derek

Lobbied for the National Horse Protection Coalition in its effort to have Congress pass the American Horse Slaughter Protection Act.

545 Cloud

The wild mustang stallion documented from birth for the PBS television series *Nature*.

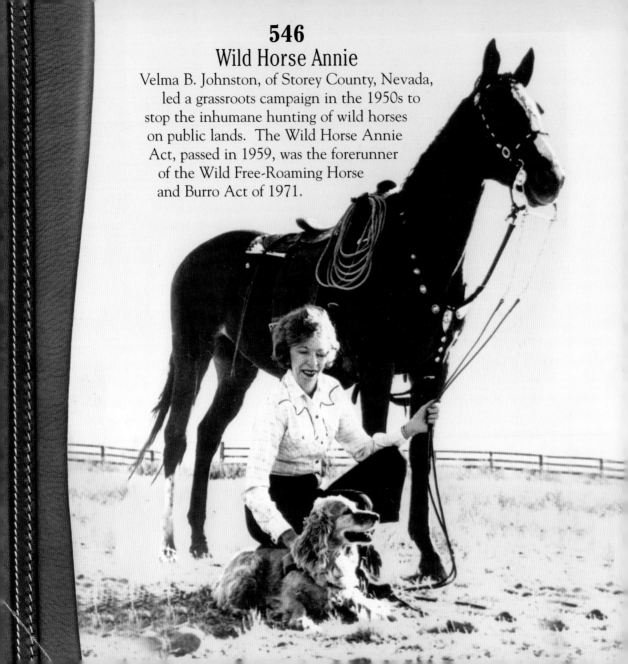

546
Wild Horse Annie

Velma B. Johnston, of Storey County, Nevada, led a grassroots campaign in the 1950s to stop the inhumane hunting of wild horses on public lands. The Wild Horse Annie Act, passed in 1959, was the forerunner of the Wild Free-Roaming Horse and Burro Act of 1971.

Wild Horses

For years wild horses have been a symbol of the spirit of the American West. At this time, an estimated forty to fifty thousand wild horses, descendants of the mounts of Spanish explorers and pioneers from centuries ago, roam Nevada, Utah, and Colorado. Due to the size of the herds and the shrinking of their feeding grounds under pressure of development and ranching, these horses are facing starvation. In an attempt to reduce the population, the government has established a Wild Horse and Burro Adoption Program, run by the Bureau of Land Management and the U.S. Forest Service.

Each year the herds are culled by approximately 15 percent, and these captured horses are brought to locations all over the United States for adoption. Anyone seeking to become a guardian of a wild horse must apply in advance and be screened in an attempt to prevent abuse. There is a minimum $125 adoption fee, but the horse does not actually become yours until you have passed a six-month inspection and had the horse at your property for one calendar year.

The auctions are open to the public. Although usually small in stature, these horses are tough and adaptable; many have gone on to great success in endurance racing, barrel racing, dressage, and jumping.

Working-Class Heroes

554
Carriage horses

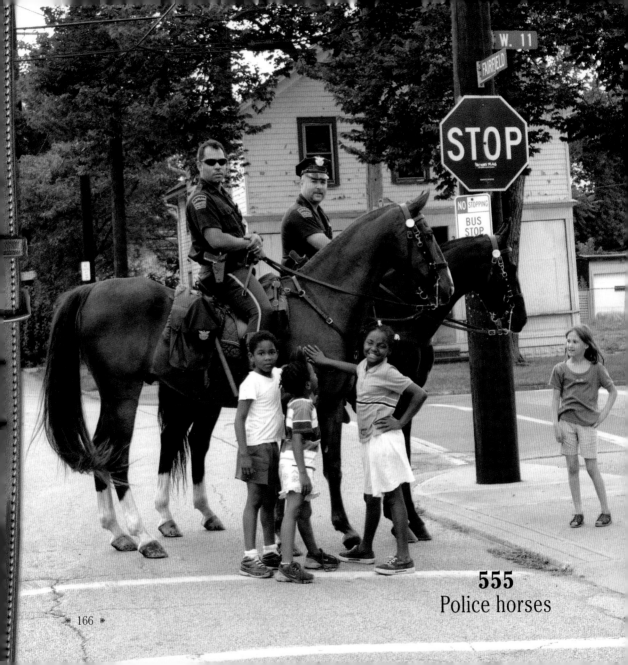

555
Police horses

556
Cavalry horses

Draft horses

These heavy horses were developed in Europe during the early medieval period, when their strength, size, and calm temperament made them ideal warhorses. This endurance and willing attitude later made them indispensable in the settling of the New World, pulling wagons, clearing land, and wielding plows. In the early 1900s many draft horses lived in cities, where they were used to pull fire trucks, trolleys, and carriages. Often dismissed as large and dull, the draft horse is actually an affectionate and loyal breed with a smooth gait, a versatile mount in the show ring, and a reliable partner in the field.

In the United States we owe a debt to the draft for not only his hours in the field but also his sacrifice in the military. The United States shipped over a million horses to Europe during World War I, only two hundred of which survived.

NORWEGIAN PLOW CO.

DUBUQUE, IOWA.

MANUFACTURERS OF

EXTRA DIAMOND HARDENED.

EASY RUNNING CAST STEEL

PLOWS.

W.C. CHAMBERLAIN, Pres't.
C.W. MITCHELL, 1st Pres't.
J. M. GRIFFITH, Vice Pres't.

GEO. STEPHENS, Sec.& Treas.
H. H. SATER, Sup't.

Clay & Co. Buffalo, N.Y.

FOUST'S HAY LOADER

Geo. M. Evans & Co.

Manufacturers of GEO. M. EVANS improved

CORN PLANTER

Cultivators, Corn plows &c.ª

No. 5 Market Street. PITTSBURGH, PA.

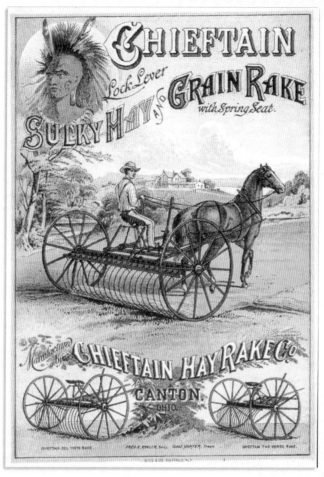

The number of draft horses in the United States has dropped steadily since the 1920s. Horses continue to be useful in agriculture and forestry, but trucks and tractors have gradually diminished the need for them.

Although today when we think of draft horses we envision either the magnificent Percherons of the Ringling Brothers Circus or the majestic Clydesdales that pull the Budweiser wagons, draft stock is experiencing a renaissance, valued for use in cross-bred hunters and pleasure horses.

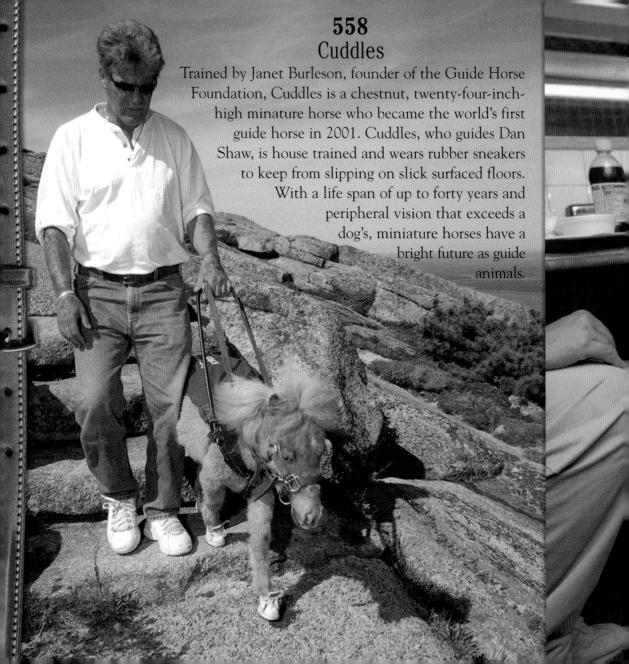

558
Cuddles

Trained by Janet Burleson, founder of the Guide Horse Foundation, Cuddles is a chestnut, twenty-four-inch-high minature horse who became the world's first guide horse in 2001. Cuddles, who guides Dan Shaw, is house trained and wears rubber sneakers to keep from slipping on slick surfaced floors. With a life span of up to forty years and peripheral vision that exceeds a dog's, miniature horses have a bright future as guide animals.

Straight from the horse's mouth

Although the horse is no longer a part of most people's daily lives,
the language of the horse is still woven into our vocabulary.

starting from scratch

This term first implied that someone was being honest in a horse race by making sure that his horse's front feet were just behind a line drawn in the dirt road that marked the race's beginning.

cavalier

This term, which now means to behave aristocratically or in a dismissive manner, once described gentlemen who rode for the military.

the inside track

On a racetrack the inside track covers the shortest distance, so the horse on the inside is at an advantage.

beating a dead horse

In racing, this means continuing to whip a horse when it obviously will not win.

taking the bit between your teeth

A horse that learns to hold the bit with its teeth renders the bit powerless, and the horse nearly unstoppable.

long in the tooth

A horse's teeth continue to grow throughout its life, so its age can be determined by their length.

putting on airs

The "airs above the ground" in classical dressage are the pinnacle of training displayed at schools like the Spanish Riding School of Vienna. To put on airs, then, is to show off a talent shared only with the elite.

chivalry

This word is derived from the French *cheval*, "horse," and refers to the gallantry of its rider, the knight.

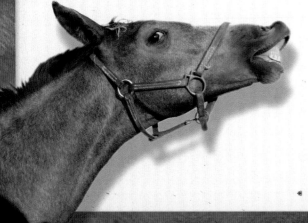

champing at the bit

An analogy to the behavior of a nervous, excited horse, which toys with its bit in its agitation.

riding roughshod

Horses are "roughshod" with nails extending out from the shoe to give them better purchase on slippery surfaces.

a wild goose chase

An Irish sport, a wild goose chase is a race where the horses stay in formation, as geese do in flight; this may refer to a course without a goal, as the order is predetermined and the race could therefore be seen as pointless.

a horse of a different color

This phrase probably originated in Shakespeare's *Twelfth Night* written in 1601.

hackneyed

Horses of the *hackney* type were often hired out and overworked; thus the word came to refer figuratively to something overused to the point of drudgery.

free rein
horse sense
hot to trot
dark horse
horse-laugh
horseplay
eat like a horse
ponytail
get off your high horse
easy in the harness
horsing around
horseless carriage
changing horses in midstream
work like a horse
getting a leg up
off and running
hoofin' it

GREAT HORSES OF TELEVISION

560 Trigger

The palomino horse in the TV series *Roy Rogers*. Trigger's registered name was Golden Cloud.

561 Target

Ridden by Annie Oakley (Gail Davis) in *Annie Oakley*

562 Buttermilk

Dale Evans's horse in *Roy Rogers*

563 Argo

The steed of Zena (Lucy Lawless) in *Zena, Warrior Princess*

564 Tornado

Ridden by Zorro (Guy Williams)

565 Penny

Ridden by Tom "Sugarfoot" Brewster (Will Hutchins) in *Sugarfoot*

566 Scout

The horse of Tonto (Jay Silverheels) in *The Lone Ranger*

567 Joker

Ridden by Andy Devine in *Wild Bill Hickock*

568 Buck

Ridden by Marshall Dillon (James Arness) in *Gunsmoke*, Buck was later sold to Lorne Greene, who rode him in *Bonanza*. Greene took Buck home at the end of the series

569 Silver

The white horse ridden by Clayton Moore as the title character in *The Lone Ranger*

570 Mr. Ed

Mr. Ed, the talking horse (whose real registered name was Bamboo Harvester), was trained by Les Hilton, also the trainer of Francis, the talking mule; Allan Lane was Mr. Ed's voice. Mr. Ed lived with his stablemate and double, Pumpkin. Some say he was trained to move his lips by putting peanut butter in his mouth; others claim he just loved to move his lips, and a monofilament had to be put across his muzzle to stop him from talking. He usually did his scenes in one take but demanded "star" treatment. Observers reported that if anyone gave the first carrot or greeting to Pumpkin, Mr. Ed would sulk and refuse to do his tricks.

571 Diablo

The Kid's (Duncan Renaldo) black-and-white paint mare in *The Cisco Kid*.

572 Loco

The palomino horse ridden by Pancho (Leo Carrillo) in *The Cisco Kid*.

573 Blaze King

Ridden by Lori Martin in the TV version of *National Velvet*.

574 Flicka

Ken McLaughlin's (Johnny Washbrook) mount at the Goosebar Ranch in *My Friend Flicka*.

575 Fury

Star of his own television series, *Fury*, this black stallion was originally named Highland Dale. Fury also appeared in the movies *Black Beauty*, *The Gypsy Colt*, *Wild Is the Wind*, and *The Return of Wildfire*, as well as in episodes of *Lassie* and *My Friend Flicka*. He earned the Patsy Award, the animal equivalent of the Oscar, for his roles in *Wild Is the Wind*, *The Gypsy Colt*, and *Fury*.

576 Topper

The mount of William Boyd in *Hopalong Cassidy*.

FAMOUS PEOPLE AND THEIR HORSES

They say it takes two to tango, or to trot. Match these famous riders with their less-well-known mounts. (answers on page 183)

Queen Elizabeth	Macaroni
Ronald Reagan	Tammen
Shirley Temple	Burmese
Caroline Kennedy	El Alamein
Bo Derek	Ligaroti
Bing Crosby	I Two Step Too
Toby McGuire	Centauro
Patrick Swayze	Uraeus
Viggo Mortensen	Seabiscuit

577 Queen Elizabeth and Burmese

A gift to the queen from the Royal Canadian Mounted Police, Burmese lived in a pasture outside Windsor Castle so the queen could see her favorite riding horse while having tea.

578 Ronald Reagan and El Alamein

A gift from the former president of Mexico, this white horse was Ronald Reagan's favorite. An accomplished horseman, Ronald Reagan did all his own horse stunts in his Western movies.

579 Shirley Temple and Seabiscuit

In 1949 Shirley Temple made a movie called *The Story of Seabiscuit*, which used actual film footage of Seabiscuit's races.

580 Caroline Kennedy and Macaroni

Macaroni, a present from Lyndon B. Johnson when J.F.K. was in office, frequently grazed on the White House lawn.

581 Bo Derek and Centauro

Centauro is one of several Andalusians owned by Bo Derek that is trained in classical dressage.

582 Bing Crosby and Ligaroti

Bing Crosby was part owner of Del Mar Racetrack and half owner with the son of Charles Howard (Seabiscuit's owner) of a racehorse named Ligaroti. In 1938 a match race was held between Seabiscuit and Ligaroti; Seabiscuit won.

583 Toby McGuire and I Two Step Too

One of nine horses who played Seabiscuit in the 2003 movie, I Two Step Too was ridden by actor Toby McGuire as jockey Red Pollard. I Two Step Too is now housed in the Barn of Breeds at the Kentucky Horse Park, Lexington, Kentucky.

584 Patrick Swayze and Tammen

Patrick Swayze breeds, rides, and shows Egyptian Arabians. His breeding stallion's name is Tammen.

585 Viggo Mortensen and Uraeus

Brego, the horse that Aragorn (Mortensen) rides in the *Lord of the Rings* movies, is played by a warm-blood stallion named Uraeus, a former FEI dressage horse trained by top international trainer Lockie Richards. Mortensen bought Uraeus at the end of filming.

For me, the concept of the perfect ride is something very personal. I wouldn't say that my life has been perfect, far from it, but the idea of the perfect ride—the hope of achieving it—has been an overriding lure, a dream that has motivated and sustained me from the first moment I mounted a horse.

—Hall of Fame jockey Gary Stevens

The Great American
Chicago June 17, 1914

The Sport of Kings

586
The Godolphin Arabian (1724–1753)
Purchased in France by Mr. Edward Coke in 1729, this stallion was acquired by
the earl of Godolphin after Coke's death and moved to the Godolphin stud
farm. His offspring included Lath and Cade and,
in the following generation, Matchem.

The Thoroughbred Foundation Sires

All modern Thoroughbred racehorses descend from three sires imported to England in the late seventeenth and early eighteenth centuries, bred to a group of horses called "the royal mares."

587 The Byerly Turk (1680–1696)

The story goes that Captain Robert Byerley captured this large black stallion from the Turks in the siege of Buda in Hungary in 1686. After his service as a warhorse, he was imported to England in 1689 and bred to a handful of mares. The resulting offspring included Herod, who became the primary sire of the continued line. The famous sire is known to this day as the Byerly Turk.

588 Darley Arabian (1700–1733)

This stallion was purchased in Syria by Thomas Darley in 1704. Imported to England, he was bred to numerous mares, resulting in the colts Flying Childers and Bartlet's Childers, but his most important descendant was his great-great-grandson Eclipse.

589 Eclipse

Eclipse was named for the total eclipse of the sun that occurred the year he was born, 1764. The last three Triple Crown winners, and the majority of all Kentucky Derby winners, trace back directly to Eclipse, and through him to the Darley Arabian.

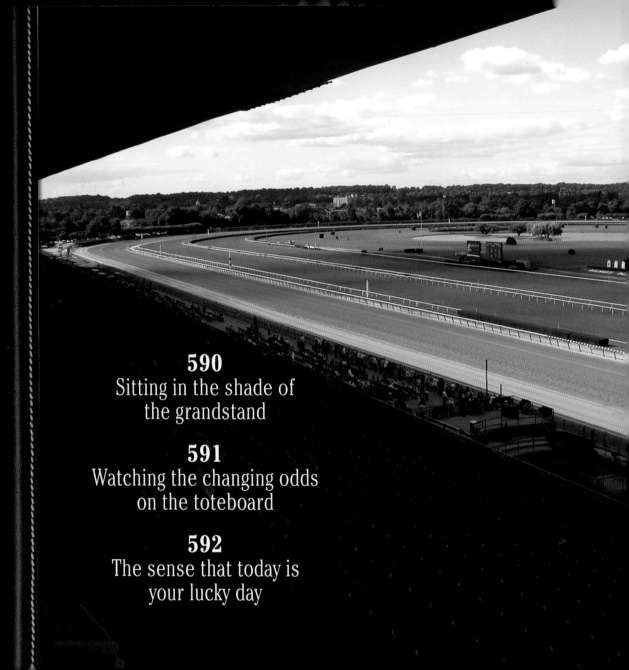

590
Sitting in the shade of
the grandstand

591
Watching the changing odds
on the toteboard

592
The sense that today is
your lucky day

AND THEY'RE OFF AND RUNNING!

Horses sometimes throw their heads and curl back their upper lips, appearing to be laughing, when introduced to a new or intriguing smell. Called a "horse-laugh," this provides a fun and serendipitous reason to place a bet.

Racing journalist Andy Beyer has developed a numerical system that rates a horse's speed by combining the horse's time in a race and the inherent speed of the track. These numbers are found exclusively in the *Daily Racing Form*.

600 Going to the morning workouts with a hot cup of coffee and the *Daily Racing Form*

601 Bandying about the phrase "Playing the ponies"

602 Placing your first exotic wager

603 Having Lady Luck on your side

604 Catching the goggles the winning jockeys throw to fans

605 Wearing lucky socks

Only a little over two minutes

Only a little over two minutes: one simultaneous metallic clash as the gates spring. Though you do not really know what it was you heard: whether it was that metallic crash, or the simultaneous thunder of the hooves in that first leap or the massed voices, the gasp, the exhalation—whatever it was, the clump of horses indistinguishable yet, like a brown wave dotted with the bright silks of the riders like chips flowing toward us along the rail until, approaching, we can begin to distinguish individuals, streaming past us now as individual horses—horses which (including the rider) once stood about eight feet tall and ten feet long, now look like arrows twice that length and less than half that thickness, shooting past and bunching again as perspective diminishes, then becoming individual horses once more around the turn into the backstretch, streaming on, to bunch for the last time into the homestretch itself, then again individuals, individual horses, the individual horse, the Horse: 2:10 4/5 minutes.

—William Faulkner

To become a millionaire in
the horse business, start with $10 million
and wait five years.
—Anonymous

Colorful jockey's silks

In the early eighteenth century, at a time when races began to be ridden by professional jockeys rather than simply the horses' owners, King Charles II told owners of horses in his races to supply their riders with distinctive colors, so he could tell whose horse was in the lead. In Roman days identifying colors had been indicated by a sash or armband, but King Charles introduced "silks"—caps and shirts worn with cream-colored breeches.

The modern-day jockey's silks that evolved from these outfits have become elaborate constructions, distinguishing themselves not only with colors but with a variety of shapes and patterns—circles, chevrons, stripes, and stars. Jockeys wear the colors of the owner they ride for in each race, so if they are riding a complete card for the day, their valet must ready perhaps ten different sets of silks. A jockey who wins several races in one day and also attends winner's-circle ceremonies must not only be a skilled rider, but also a quick-change artist.

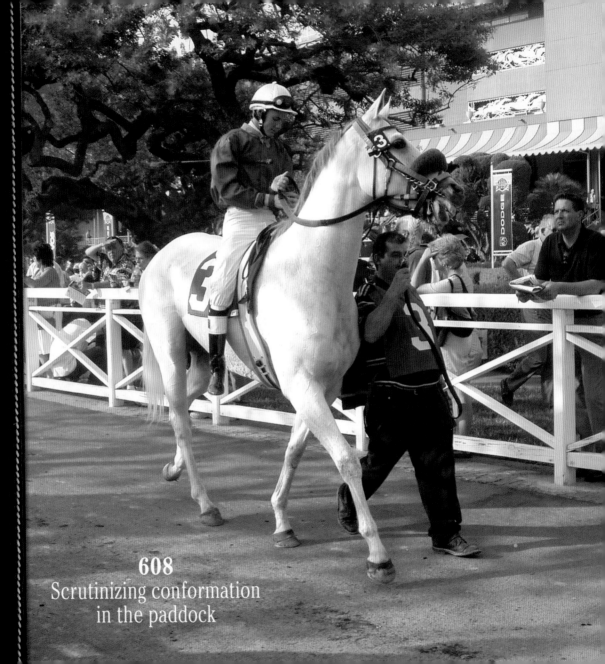

608
Scrutinizing conformation
in the paddock

MAN O' WAR

Born on March 29, 1917, by Fair Play, out of Mahubah, this gangly, extra-long-legged foal is arguably the best racehorse that history has known. His breeder, August Belmont II, sold his entire crop of yearlings before leaving for World War I. The big red colt was a favorite, and prior to the sale Belmont's wife named him "My Man O' War" in honor of her husband. Samuel Riddle purchased the colt and turned him over to his trainer, Louis Feustil.

Fuestil had his hands full, as this rangy colt, nicknamed "Big Red," proved to have a temperament as large as his size. Through patient training, Man O'War made his debut as a two-year-old at Belmont Park. He won easily by six lengths and was moved up in class to stakes races. In twenty-one starts, Man O'War had twenty wins and one second, setting three world records, two American records, and three track records. He became so feared by his competitors that in one stakes race only one horse came to challenge him, a horse named Hoodwink—and hoodwinked he was, losing by a hundred lengths.

> ## He wuz de mostest hoss.
> —Will Harbut, longtime groom and companion of Man O'War

Man O'War's only defeat was to a horse aptly named Upset in the Stanford Memorial Stakes at Saratoga in 1919. The starting gate had yet to be invented, and races began with horses milling around at the starting line, waiting for the flag to fall. "Big Red" was in his usual feisty form, and after five false starts, the flag was dropped while jockey Louis Loftus had Man O'War sideways at the line. It was a bad start, and Man O'War was pocketed on the rail by Golden Broom. Running wide in a six-furlong race, Man O'War simply ran out of track before he could catch Upset. This race immortalized Upset, but Man O'War went on to beat him five times in his career.

Samuel Riddle refused to enter Man O'War in the Kentucky Derby, and although "Big Red" went on to win the Preakness and the Belmont that year, he couldn't claim a Triple Crown. When Jockey Club handicappers decided that Man O'War would have to carry 140–45 pounds the following season, Samuel Riddle retired the horse to stud. In his second career, Man O'War produced sixty-four stakes winners, including War Admiral.

623
Saratoga Race Course
Nicknamed "the Spa," this is the oldest North American racetrack still in existence, opened in 1864.

624 The filigree shadows cast by weeping willows

625 Sunrise breakfast each race day on the clubhouse porch

626 The "country fair" atmosphere of the vendor booths

627 Cheerful red-and-white-striped awnings and wrought-iron racing friezes

628 A casual lunch by the carousel

629 Choosing champagne and crab cakes, or a furlong frank and cotton candy

630 Hobnobbing with the racing elite

631 Getting box seats for the Travers Stakes, the "Midsummer Derby"

632 Peering into the glassed-in display of jockey silks

633 Pony Tales, the bookstore under the grandstand

Asked directions to Saratoga Springs from New York City, *New York Times* sports columnist Red Smith replied, "Drive north about 175 miles and go back 100 years."

634 White breeches, scarlet tails, and brass bugles with the call to the post

635 Friendly track ponies

636 Tables by the window

637 The roar of the crowd

638 Surrounding yourself with racing legends at the Breeders' Cup World Thoroughbred Championships
Once a year a race card is put together of the best of the best from around the world in each division of flat racing. The Breeders' Cup moves to a different racetrack each year.

639 A horse in the program with the same name as your ex-boyfriend, great-aunt, or family dog
The winner of the 1956 Kentucky Derby and Belmont Stakes was named Needles because, as a sickly foal, he received so many injections.

640 Watching your horse win all over again on instant replay

BREEDERS' CUP

653
Going to the track on
opening day

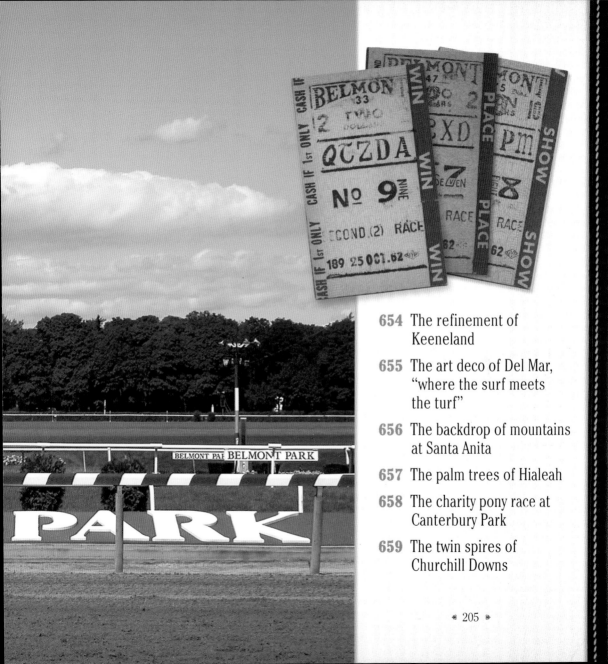

660
Sharing a tip
with another railbird

THE KENTUCKY DERBY

Gold Derby Trophy exclusively designed by

LEMON & SON
FOURTH AVENUE AT CHESTNUT
JEWELERS SINCE 1828

665 Kentucky Derby trophy

The coveted gold Kentucky Derby trophy was first presented in 1924 to Mrs. Rosa Hoots, owner of Derby winner Black Gold. Its basic design remained unchanged until the running of the 125th Kentucky Derby in 1999, when Derby officials deferred to racing lore and flipped the horseshoe on the cup so the points were skyward in order to keep "luck" from running out.

666 Kentucky Derby roses

Each year a garland of red roses is placed over the withers of the Kentucky Derby winner. The rose has become synonymous with the Derby, but it was not deemed the official flower until 1896, and that year the roses were pink and white. In 1904 the red rose became the official flower, and in 1925 sports columnist Bill Corum coined the phrase "the run for the roses."

667 Watching the garland being constructed at Kroger's on the eve of the Derby

The Derby's garland of roses is stitched into a green satin backing each year in public view at a Kroger's store.

668 Betting on the beautiful gray horse against all odds

Handicappers will tell you to never bet on the gray horse, as he is usually the crowd favorite of the novice, and the horse's odds will collapse at post time.

669 Kentucky Derby winners who were gray

Determine (1954)
Decidedly (1962; son of Determine)
Spectacular Bid (1979)
Gato Del Sol (1982)
Winning Colors (1988)
Silver Charm (1997)
Monarchos (2001)

Silver Charm and Gary Stevens with
the Kentucky Derby roses, 1997

Trainer Bob Baffert congratulates
Gary Stevens who won the 1997
Kentucky Derby riding Silver Charm.

670
Jockeys who have won the most Kentucky Derbies

Eddie Arcaro (5), Bill Hartack (5), Bill Shoemaker (4), Isaac Murphy (3), Angel Cordero Jr. (3), Earl Sande (3), Gary Stevens (3)

671
Trainers who have won the most Kentucky Derbies

Ben Jones (6), H. J. Thompson (4), D. Wayne Lukas (4), Bob Baffert (3), Sunny Jim Fitzsimmons (3), Max Hirsch (3)

672
Oldest jockey to win the Kentucky Derby

Bill Shoemaker, age 54, rode Ferdinand in 1986. Shoemaker was also the oldest, at 56, to win a Breeders' Cup race, winning the 1987 Classic with Ferdinand.

673
Youngest jockeys to win the Kentucky Derby

Alonzo Clayton, age 15, rode Azra in 1892. James Perkins, age 15, rode Halma in 1895.

674 **African-American jockeys who have won the Derby (and their mounts)**

Oliver Lewis, 1875 (Aristides)

William Walker, 1877 (Baden-Baden)

George G. Lewis, 1880 (Fonso)

Babe Hurd, 1882 (Apollo)

Isaac Murphy, 1884 (Buchanan), 1890 (Riley), and 1891 (Kingman).

Murphy was the first jockey to win three Kentucky Derbies.

Erskine Henderson, 1885 (Joe Cotton)

Isaac Lewis, 1887 (Montrose)

Alonzo Clayton, 1892 (Azra)

James Perkins, 1895 (Halma)

Willie Simms, 1896 (Ben Brush) and 1898 (Plaudit).

Jimmy Winkfield, 1901 (His Eminence) and 1902 (Alan-a-Dale).

675 **Fillies who have won the Kentucky Derby**

Regret (1915)

Genuine Risk (1980)

Winning Colors (1988)

676 **Kentucky Derby winners owned by Calumet Farms**

Whirlaway (1941)

Pensive (1944)

Citation (1948)

Ponder (1949)

Hill Gail (1952)

Iron Liege (1957)

Tim Tam (1958)

Forward Pass (1968)

677 Derby winners who have sired Derby winners

FATHER	SON
Halma (1895)	Alan-a-Dale (1902)
Bubbling Over (1926)	Burgoo King (1932)
Gallant Fox (1930)	Omaha (1935)
Reigh Count (1928)	Count Fleet (1943)
Bold Venture (1936)	Assault (1946)
Pensive (1944)	Ponder (1949)
Bold Venture (1936)	Middleground (1950)
Count Fleet (1943)	Count Turf (1951)
Ponder (1949)	Needles (1956)
Determine (1954)	Decidedly (1962)
Swaps (1955)	Chateaugay (1963)
Seattle Slew (1977)	Swale (1984)
Unbridled (1990)	Grindstone (1996)

Gallant Fox, 1930

Omaha, 1935

The 1942 Kentucky Derby

678
The Mint Julep

There are various recipes for the famous mint julep, but what is really important is that it is made with the ceremony and spirit that the occasion deserves.

Mint Julep Recipe

On the morning of the eve of the Kentucky Derby, step outdoors and pick a cup of sprigs of fresh mint with the morning dew clinging to the leaves. Inhale the aroma as you walk back inside.

Boil one cup of fresh spring water with one cup of sugar without stirring. Add a handful of fresh mint leaves, gently bruised, to the syrup. Pour the concoction into a closed container and refrigerate overnight while making your final Derby preparations or attending a Derby Ball.

When you are ready to imbibe, take out a silver mint-julep cup or an eight-ounce tumbler. Pick more fresh mint. Lay three or four fresh leaves in the bottom of your glass and fill with crushed ice. Add one tablespoon of your refrigerated syrup, one tablespoon of spring water, and two ounces of good Kentucky bourbon. Stir, sip, and enjoy.

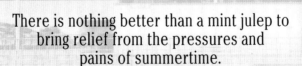

There is nothing better than a mint julep to bring relief from the pressures and pains of summertime.

—Truman Capote

679 Having a Derby sandwich with the "trackies" at Wagner's Pharmacy in Louisville

Wagner's Pharmacy, located across the street from Churchill Downs, is a drugstore and grill with wall-to-wall finish line photos from the Kentucky Derby. The pharmacy sells their own version of the collectible Derby glass, but rather than the winner, their glass records the name of the horse that finished last in the Derby.

680 Savoring your first bite of the original Derby-Pie®

Derby-Pie® was first served at the Melrose Inn in Prospect, Kentucky half a century ago. Now a registered trademark of Kern's Kitchen, Inc., the pie is a mouthwatering confection of walnuts and chocolate. Kern's Kitchen is a small family-run operation established by George Kern, the previous manager of the Melrose Inn restaurant. The recipe is a secret, but George's mother, Leaudra, will tell you how to serve it—warm from the oven and topped with real whipped cream.

681 Sipping Black-eyed Susans at the Preakness

682 Drinking White Carnations or a Belmont Breeze at the Belmont Stakes

683
Hoping that every Derby winner will become a Triple Crown champion

This Kentucky Derby, whatever it is—a race, an emotion, a turbulence, an explosion—is one of the most beautiful and violent and satisfying things I have ever experienced. I am glad I have seen and felt it at last.

—John Steinbeck

THE TRIPLE CROWN

The holy grail of Thoroughbred racing, the Triple Crown
is composed of the Kentucky Derby, the Preakness, and the Belmont.

	OWNER	TRAINER	JOCKEY
684	**J. K. L. ROSS**	**GUY BEDWELL**	**JOHNNY LOFTUS**
	## Sir Barton		
	ch.c., Star Shoot-Lady Sterling by Hanover, bred by John E. Madden & Gooch Madden, Kentucky **(1919)**		
685	**BELAIR STUD**	**JAMES FITZSIMMONS**	**EARL SANDE**
	## Gallant Fox		
	b.c., Sir Gallahad II-Marguerite by Celt, bred by Belair Stud, Kentucky **(1930)**		
686	**BELAIR STUD**	**JAMES FITZSIMMONS**	**WILLIAM SAUNDERS**
	## Omaha		
	ch.c., Gallant Fox-Flambino by Wrack, bred by Belair Stud, Kentucky **(1935)**		
687	**GLEN RIDDLE FARM**	**GEORGE CONWAY**	**CHARLIE KURTSINGER**
	## War Admiral		
	br.c., Man O'War-Brushup by Sweep, bred by Samuel D. Riddle, Kentucky **(1937)**		
688	**CALUMET FARM**	**BEN A. JONES**	**EDDIE ARCARO**
	## Whirlaway		
	ch.c., Blenheim-Dustwhirl by Sweep, bred by Calumet Farm, Lexington, Kentucky **(1941)**		

OWNER	TRAINER	JOCKEY

689

MRS. JOHN D. HERTZ   G. D. CAMERON   JOHN LONGDEN

Count Fleet

br.c., Reigh Count-Quickly by Haste, bred by Mrs. John D. Hertz, Kentucky

(1943)

690

KING RANCH   MAX HIRSCH   WARREN MEHRTENS

Assault

b.c., Bold Venture-Igual by Equipoise, bred by King Ranch, Texas

(1946)

691

CALUMET FARM   BEN A. JONES   EDDIE ARCARO

Citation

br.c, Bull Lea-Hydroplane II by Hyperion, bred by Calumet Farm, Kentucky

(1948)

692

MEADOW STABLE   LUCIEN LAURIN   RON TURCOTTE

Secretariat

ch.c., Bold Ruler-Somethingroyal by Princequillo, bred by Meadow Stud, Inc., Virginia

(1973)

693

KAREN L. TAYLOR   WILLIAM H. TURNER, JR.   JEAN CRUGUET

Seattle Slew

br.c., Bold Reasoning-My Charmer by Poker, bred by Ben S. Castleman, Kentucky

(1977)

694

HARBOR VIEW FARM   LAZARO BARRERA   STEVE CAUTHEN

Affirmed

ch.c., Exclusive Native-Won't Tell You by Crafty Admiral, bred by Harbor View Farm, Florida

(1978)

SECRETARIAT

Secretariat looked the part of the American hero he was to become. A vivid red colt with impeccable conformation, a white star and snip, and three white stockings, he wore the brilliant blue-and-white-checkered hood and silks of Meadow Stable. Sired by the famous Bold Ruler out of Somethingroyal, he earned for himself the nickname first carried by Man O'War, "Big Red."

As a two-year-old in 1972, Secretariat lost his first race at Aqueduct, getting bumped at the gate and swerving in traffic. A fast learner, he went on to win the Sanford Stakes, the Hopeful Stakes, the Belmont Futurity, the Laurel Futurity, and the Garden State Stakes. He was named Horse of the Year that year, only the third two-year-old to be given that honor, and the first to win it by a unanimous vote.

The 3–2 favorite going into the Kentucky Derby, Secretariat ran from the back and closed in on horse after horse to win by two and a half lengths in the record time of 1:59 2/5 for a mile and a quarter. The first horse to run the Derby in less than two minutes, he also ran each quarter-mile faster than the one before. In the Preakness he again won by two and a half lengths; he was clocked at 1:53 2/5, but the official timer reported 1:55. To this day there is controversy over Secretariat's actual time.

The media frenzy was high for the Belmont, but even hopes for the first Triple Crown winner in twenty-five years failed to prepare anyone for the experience to follow. As jockey Ron Turcotte broke from the gate, Secretariat lunged for the lead with Sham and battled with him for six furlongs. He then soared ahead to a ten-furlong lead in the mid-backstretch, twelve by the turn, and an amazing thirty-one lengths ahead at the finish. Even the television's wide-angle lens couldn't capture both the winner passing the finish line and the other horses in the pack. A new record was set for running 1 1/4 miles—1:59 flat.

Secretariat appeared on the cover of *Time*, *Newsweek*, and *Sports Illustrated* all in the same week, won back-to-back Horse of the Year titles, and was given number thirty-five on the list of Greatest Athletes of the Twentieth Century, the only non-human on the list.

Secretariat winning the
Kentucky Derby in 1973

696
Watching history
unfold

697
Racing lingo

As with any sport, part of the fun of racing is the instant camaraderie with perfect strangers that a shared passion gives you. There's nothing like leaning on the rail, exchanging hot tips with another "railbird," if you can talk the talk.

clerk of scales: *the official who weighs the jockeys before and after the race*

daylight: *an opening between horses wide enough to squeeze through*

four-bagger: *a jockey who wins four races on one day's card*

going wide: *running around the pack rather than through it*

hot box: *the sauna the jockeys use to make weight*

rate: *hold a horse back to conserve his speed*

scratch: *withdraw a previously entered horse from a race*

stone-cold loser: *a horse that comes in last*

closer: *a horse whose preferred strategy is to stay to the back and come to the front later in the race*

stalker: *a horse who runs best when just behind the leader in the race*

quinella: *a bet where you pick the first and second horse in either order*

bug boy: *an apprentice jockey*

plater: *a claiming horse*

tote board: *a display in the infield that shows current odds on entries*

stud book: *a registry and genealogical record of Thoroughbreds maintained by the Jockey Club*

blue hen: *an influential broodmare*

Dagwood sandwich: *Putting money down on every horse with midrange odds*

track bias: *a racing surface that favors a certain running style*

spitting the bit: *when an exhausted horse has given up pulling on the bit to run*

pinhooker: *someone who buys a young racehorse specifically to resell it for a profit*

hotwalker: *a person who walks horses to cool them down after workouts or races*

in the money: *a horse who comes in first, second, or third*

maiden: *a horse that has not won a race*

morning line: *probable odds on each horse in a race determined by the track handicapper*

flatten out: *to slow down*

clubhouse turn: *the first turn on the track after the finish line*

bridge jumper: *player who "bets the farm" on a favorite to show, only to see him finish up the track*

finishing up the track: *ending the race behind those in the money*

claiming race: *a race in which each horse entered can be purchased for a set price before the race—for example, a $20,000 claiming race*

cuppy: *used to describe a dry but loose racing surface that shows hoofprints*

clocker: *one who records the time at races and workouts*

breeze: *to work a horse at moderate speed*

chalk: *the wagering favorite in a race (when odds were kept on blackboards, a horse would "get a lot of chalk")*

overlay: *a horse going off at higher odds than its past performances would merit*

across the board: *betting a horse to win, place, and show*

the wheel: *a wager combining a favorite horse with all other horses entered*

Daily Double: *a wager where you pick the winner in two specified consecutive races*

exacta: *a wager where you pick the first and second horses in exact order*

exacta box: *wagering on an exacta in either order*

trifecta: *a wager where you must pick the first, second, and third horse in exact order*

Pick Six: *picking the winner in six consecutive races*

post time: *the designated time the race should start*

silks: *the owner's racing colors worn by the jockey in the race*

washed out: *when a horse is lathered up prior to the race, indicating poor conditioning*

shows early speed: *likes to take the lead immediately in a race*

SEATTLE SLEW

In 1977 Seattle Slew became the tenth winner of the Triple Crown. Purchased for only $17,500 by a logger, an airline stewardess, and a veterinarian and his wife, Seattle Slew—by Bold Reasoning, out of My Charmer—was a bargain because he had been born with a misshapen hoof. When the owners turned

Seattle Slew over to their trainer, Bill Turner, he nicknamed Slew "Baby Huey" due to the awkward way he ran, throwing one foot to the side.

Seattle Slew didn't venture onto the track until late in his two-year-old year, in September, 1976. He won his first three races, rested over the winter, and won again the next season.

On the day of the Kentucky Derby, Slew was the hands-down favorite. When he broke from the gate, he swerved and collided with Get the Axe, but he quickly recovered and, though he'd started at the back of the pack, went on to lead by three lengths in the stretch.

Two weeks later, in the Preakness, his time was 1:54 2/5, beating Secretariat's original timed record and grazing the unofficial record. On the day of the Belmont, Seattle Slew was faced with a muddy track for the first time in his career, but he led wire-to-wire and won by four lengths.

Seattle Slew's owners wanted to continue to campaign their horse on the West Coast. Trainer Bill Turner felt that Slew needed a rest, but the owners were determined: he ran at Hollywood Park in the Swaps Stakes, only to come in fourth.

Although Seattle Slew had been named Champion Two-Year-Old and Horse of the Year as a three-year-old and was the first undefeated Triple Crown winner, the owners fired their trainer and hired Doug Peterson. Seattle Slew contracted a life-threatening virus and could not race until the following May. In 1978 he beat Triple Crown winner Affirmed in the Marlboro Cup, and at the end of the racing season was retired to stud. Seattle Slew died at twenty-eight, exactly twenty-five years from the date he won the Kentucky Derby.

Trainer Charlie Whittingham holds the reins of Kentucky Derby winner Ferdinand, May 16, 1986. Jockey Bill Shoemaker, age 54, was the oldest jockey ever to win the Derby.

LEGENDARY TRAINERS

699 Woody Stephens

Stephens trained an unprecedented five consecutive Belmont Stakes winners, two Derby winners (Cannonade and Swale), and one Preakness winner. He received the Eclipse Award in 1983.

700 "Sunny Jim" Fitzsimmons

In addition to two Triple Crown winners, Gallant Fox and Omaha, Fitzsimmons also trained Nashua, Bold Ruler, and Granville.

701 Charlie Whittingham

Eclipse Award winner in 1971, 1982, and 1989, Whittingham trained Ferdinand, Sunday Silence, and Ack Ack. He was the top money earner for seven years.

702 Ben A. Jones

The trainer for Calumet Farms, Ben Jones trained six Kentucky Derby winners, including two Triple Crown winners, Citation and Whirlaway.

GREAT JOCKEYS

703 Tod "Yankee Doodle Dandy" Sloan
Famous for his 1897 innovation— riding above the saddle with shortened stirrup leathers—Sloan had an amazing 30 percent winning average and three times won five of six races on a daily card.

704 Earle "the Handy Guy" Sande
Sande won the Triple Crown on Gallant Fox, but considered Man O'War his best mount.

705 George "Iceman" Woolf
Woolf, who rode Seabiscuit in the famous match race with War Admiral, died from injuries sustained in a race at Santa Anita in 1946. The George Woolf Award, recognizing jockeys who have had a significant impact on the sport, was established in his honor.

706 Ted Atkinson, "the Professor"
Atkinson was the first jockey to surpass one million dollars in winnings, in 1946.

707 Johnny Longden
Longden, who won the Triple Crown in 1945 on Count Fleet, is the only person to win the Kentucky Derby both as a jockey and as a trainer (with Majestic Prince). In addition to winning the George Woolf Award, he was given the Special Eclipse Award in 1994.

708 Eddie Arcaro "the Master"
Perhaps the greatest jockey of all time, Eddie Arcaro won five Kentucky Derbies, six Preaknesses, and six Belmonts. He claimed the Triple Crown with both Whirlaway and Citation. Eleven of his mounts became Horse of the Year.

709 Bill Hartack
Hartack won five Kentucky Derbies, three Preaknesses, and one Belmont.

Eddie Arcaro, Whirlaway, and trainer
Ben Jones at the Kentucky Derby, 1941

710 Bill "the Shoe" Shoemaker

His four Kentucky Derbies, two Preaknesses, five Belmont Stakes, eleven Santa Anita Handicaps, and eight Santa Anita Derbies garnered Shoemaker the George Woolf Award and the Eclipse Award in 1976 and 1981.

711 Chris McCarron

The winner of two Derbies, two Preaknesses, three Belmonts, and three Breeders' Cup Classics, McCarron received the Eclipse Award twice, in 1974 and 1980, as well as the George Woolf Award.

712 Jerry Bailey

Bailey won the Eclipse Award in 1995, 1996, 1997 and 1999, and won four Breeders' Cup Classics during a five year period from 1991 through 1995.

713 Gary Stevens

Stevens, who played George Woolf in the movie *Seabiscuit*, in his own right won three Derbies, two Preaknesses, eight Breeders' Cup races, and the Dubai Cup. He received the Eclipse Award in 1998.

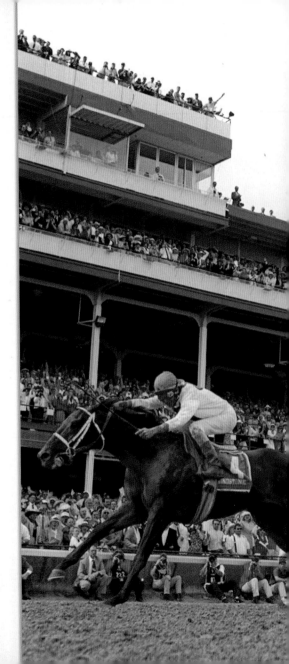

Jerry Bailey (left) rides Grindstone to a photo finish in the 122nd Kentucky Derby, May 4, 1996. Chris McCarron, aboard Cavonnier (right), was second.

A. P. Indy	Black Helen	Count Fleet	Firenze
Ack Ack	Blue Larkspur	Crusader	Flatterer
Affectionately	Bold 'n Determined	Dahlia	Flawlessly
Affirmed	Bold Ruler	Damascus	Foolish Pleasure
All Along	Bon Nouvel	Dark Mirage	Forego
Alsab	Boston	Davona Dale	Fort Marcy
Alydar	Broomstick	Desert Vixen	Gallant Bloom
Alysheba	Buckpasser	Devil Diver	Gallant Fox
American Eclipse	Busher	Discovery	Gallant Man
Armed	Bushranger	Domino	Gallorette
Artful	Cafe Prince	Dr. Fager	Gamely
Arts and Letters	Carry Back	Easy Goer	Genuine Risk
Assault	Cavalcade	Eight Thirty	Go for Wand
Battleship	Challedon	Elkridge	Good and Plenty
Bayakoa	Chris Evert	Emperor of Norfolk	Granville
Bed o'Roses	Cicada	Equipoise	Grey Lag
Beldame	Cigar	Exceller	Gun Bow
Ben Brush	Citation	Exterminator	Hamburg
Bewitch	Coaltown	Fair Play	Hanover
Bimelech	Colin	Fairmount	Henry of Navarre
Black Gold	Commando	Fashion	Hill Prince

Hindoo	Myrtlewood	Reigh Count	Stymie
Holy Bull	Nashua	Riva Ridge	Sun Beau
Imp	Native Dancer	Roamer	Sunday Silence
Jay Trump	Native Diver	Roseben	Susan's Girl
John Henry	Needles	Round Table	Swaps
Johnstown	Neji	Ruffian	Sword Dancer
Jolly Roger	Noor	Ruthless	Sysonby
Kelso	Northern Dancer	Salvator	Ta Wee
Kentucky	Oedipus	Sarazen	Ten Broeck
Kingston	Old Rosebud	Seabiscuit	Tim Tam
La Prevoyante	Omaha	Searching	Tom Fool
Lady's Secret	Pan Zareta	Seattle Slew	Top Flight
L'Escargot	Parole	Secretariat	Tosmah
Lexington	Paseana	Serena's Song	Twenty Grand
Longfellow	Personal Ensign	Shuvee	Twilight Tear
Luke Blackburn	Peter Pan	Silver Spoon	Two Lea
Majestic Prince	Precisionist	Sir Archy	War Admiral
Man O' War	Princess Doreen	Sir Barton	Whirlaway
Maskette	Princess Rooney	Skip Away	Whisk Broom II
Miesque	Real Delight	Slew o'Gold	Winning Colors
Miss Woodford	Regret	Spectacular Bid	Zaccio
			Zev

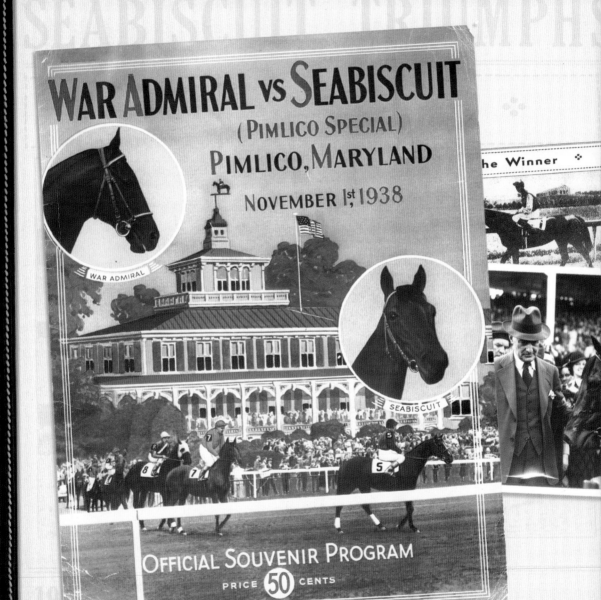

WAR ADMIRAL VS SEABISCUIT

(PIMLICO SPECIAL)

PIMLICO, MARYLAND

NOVEMBER 1st, 1938

WAR ADMIRAL

SEABISCUIT

the Winner

OFFICIAL SOUVENIR PROGRAM

PRICE **50** CENTS

Great Match Races

A match race is a head-to-head race between two rivals to settle for once and all which is faster.

715 Man O'War – Sir Barton (1920)

Man O'War's last race was won by seven lengths over Triple Crown winner Sir Barton.

716 Seabiscuit–War Admiral (1938)

Seabiscuit, a small, ordinary-looking West Coast horse who loved to overeat and sleep in his stall, won the hearts of Americans during the Great Depression due to his indomitable spirit and the brilliant campaigning of his owner, Charles Howard. Howard, along with trainer Tom Smith and jockey Red Pollard, were threads in a tapestry of the American dream come to life. Seabiscuit challenged War Admiral in a match race on War Admiral's home track, Pimlico, winning by four lengths although his regular jockey, Red Pollard, due to an injury had been replaced by George Woolf.

717 Alsab – Whirlaway (1942)

In a photo finish, Alsab beat older Triple Crown winner Whirlaway at Narragansett Park, Rhode Island.

718 Armed – Assault (1947)

Calumet's Armed came home eight lengths ahead of Triple Crown winner Assault at Pimlico. Armed, a gelding, began his career as a track pony.

719 Nashua – Swaps (1955)

Swaps beat Nashua in the 1955 Kentucky Derby, but lost to him in their match race at Washington Park the same year.

720 Foolish Pleasure – Ruffian (1975)

Ruffian did not run in the 1975 Kentucky Derby due to a hairline fracture. In July she challenged the Derby winner, Foolish Pleasure, to a match race. Ruffian, in the lead, broke down, snapping her leg, but refused to quit running. Despite heroic efforts to save her, she had to be put down the next day.

LEGENDARY HORSE FARMS

721 Calumet Farms

In 1924, William Monroe Wright, founder of Calumet Baking Powder, established this legendary Thoroughbred breeding farm originally for standardbreds. In its long list of achievements, winning eight Kentucky Derbies and two Triple Crowns, it also carries the distinction of being the only farm to win both the Hambletonian and the Kentucky Derby.

722 Claiborne Farms

Birthplace of Seabiscuit, Forego, Kelso, Claiborne has foaled seventeen Horse of the Year winners.

723 Coolmore

A premier stud farm, based in Ireland, Coolmore also has farms in Kentucky and Australia.

724 Juddmonte

Consists of three farms in the United States and six farms in Ireland and England. Named the Eclipse Champion Breeder of the Year 2001, 2002, 2003.

725 Spendthrift Farm

Home of Nashua and other leading sires, Spendthrift Farms and owner, Leslie Combs, were the top sellers at the Keeneland yearling sales for 15 consecutive years, 1949–1963.

726 Three Chimneys

"The idea is excellence" is the slogan of this premier breeding farm, home to Seattle Slew for 17 years, and now housing such celebrities as Point Given, Dynaformer, and Smarty Jones.

Seattle Slew's
barn cat roams
the grounds of
Three Chimneys

Julie Krone

Great Women in Racing

727 Helen Hay Whitney
Known as "the First Lady of the Turf," Mrs. Whitney was the first woman owner to win the Kentucky Derby twice, in 1931 and 1942.

728 Mary Hirsch
The first woman trainer licensed in the United States (in 1934, in Illinois and Michigan), in 1937 Hirsch, daughter of famed trainer Max Hirsch, became the first female trainer of a Kentucky Derby horse, No Sir.

Jenine Sahadi

729 Diane Crump
The first woman jockey to ride in a parimutuel race in North America, in 1969.

730 Jenine Sahadi
Sahadi is the only woman trainer to win a Breeders' Cup race (the 1996 Sprint), with Lit de Justice; she won the Sprint again with Elmhurst in 1997, and won the prestigious Santa Anita Derby in 2000 with The Deputy.

731 Julie Krone
Krone is both the only female jockey to win a Triple Crown race (with Colonial Affair, at the 1993 Belmont Stakes) and the only female jockey to win a Breeders' Cup race (the 2003 Juvenile Fillies, with Halfbridled).

CECIL RALEIGH & SEYMOUR HICKS' GREAT ENGLISH PLAY **SPORTING**

"LADY LOVE" WINS THE DERBY. THE MOST EXCITING AND REALISTIC H
SHOWING **EPSOM DOWNS**, THE G
GALLANT VICTORY OF THE BEAUTIFUL THOROUGHBRED "LADY LOVE" MAKING IN ALL THE MOS

LIFE

JACOB LITT
PROPRIETOR.

THE
STROBRIDGE
LITH. CO.
CINCINNATI & NEW YORK

...CE EVER PRESENTED ON THE STAGE.
...GLISH RACE TRACK ON DERBY DAY, AND THE
...D, AND ANIMATED STAGE PICTURE EVER SEEN.

Racing Around the World

England's Triple Crown

732 The Two Thousand Guineas

This one-mile race for three-year-olds is held each May at Newmarket, Suffolk

733 The Epsom Derby

A one-and-a-half-mile race for three-year-olds held in June at Epsom Downs, in Epsom, Surrey

734 The St. Leger Stakes

Held each September at Doncaster, Yorkshire, this is a one-and-three-quarter-mile race for three-year-olds

735 West Australian

In 1853 West Australian was the first English Triple Crown winner. The next year he won the Gold Cup (two and a half miles), after winning a two-mile race the day before!

736 Wearing a fabulous hat to Ascot

Although the Ascot racecourse in Berkshire, England, is open year-round, the Ascot meet in June is the major event of the social calendar. Due to continued royal patronage, this race meet is filled with tradition and pageantry, sophisticated fashion and the who's who of Britain. The Ascot meet was immortalized in *My Fair Lady*, when Eliza Doolittle elegantly leaned over the rail and yelled, "Move your bloody arse!"

737 Brown Jack

A beloved racehorse in England in the 1930s, Brown Jack won the Queen Alexandra Stakes at Ascot in six consecutive years.

738 Queen Anne

Passionate about racing, Queen Anne was the first monarch to race at York; she established Queen's Plate races at several courses, the winners of which were awarded 100 pounds.

739 The Grand National

740 Moifaa

The ship bringing Moifaa from New Zealand for the Grand National sank in a storm outside Liverpool. Days later he was found by a fisherman, who returned him to his owner. Moiffa had swum 50 miles to the safety of an uninhabited island. He went on to win the 1904 Grand National.

Ascot

MEMBERS' ENCLOSURE

Saturday 13th July

2002

No 2349

RED RUM

A strapping red bay, "Rummie," as his fans liked to call him, was a national hero. The only horse ever to win three Grand Nationals, he came in second in two more.

Originally bred to be a flat racer, by Quorum, out of Mared, Red Rum was first purchased with his stablemate, Curlicue, for four hundred pounds. He ran his first flat race at Aintree, home of the Grand National, teamed with Curlicue. Giving an unusual start to an amazing career, the two stablemates tied in a dead heat.

"Rummie" ran his first Grand National in 1973, chal-lenging the favorite, Crisp. He not only won the steeplechase but set a speed record of 9 minutes and 1.9 seconds that held for sixteen years. He beat Crisp by a margin of only three-quarters of a length, but the two of them left the rest of the field twenty-five lengths behind.

Red Rum returned as the favorite to Aintree

> "Rummie" ran his first Grand National in 1973, challenging the favorite, Crisp. He not only won the steeplechase but set a speed record of 9 minutes and 1.9 seconds that held for sixteen years.

for the National in 1974, only to have handicappers weigh him down with an amazing 170 pounds. Even carrying this weight, Red Rum finished ahead of L'Escargot by seven lengths. In 1975 Red Rum came in second to L'Escargot. In 1976, he again came in second, this time to Rag Tag.

Twelve years old in 1977, "Rummie" attempted the National one more time. With Tommie Stack in the saddle, he won by an astounding twenty-five lengths. In 1978, he injured his heel just prior to the race.

Red Rum lived out the rest of his life as a national celebrity, making special appearances at a variety of events and with fans visiting daily at his stable. He was brought back to Aintree racecourse to celebrate his thirtieth birthday and died shortly thereafter. Red Rum is buried at the finish line pole of the Grand National.

742 Longchamp

The premier French racecourse, Longchamp, in the Bois de Boulogne, Paris, hosts only turf races. The course is a complex web of tracks, rather than a simple oval. There is a windmill at the clubhouse turn, and a hill is built into a portion of the track. Be careful which way you look; the horses run clockwise.

743 Prix de l'Arc de Triomphe

A mile-and-a-half race for colts and fillies three years and up, the Arc de Triomphe is held at Longchamp the first Sunday of October

744 The Grand Steeplechase de Paris

A spectacular steeplechase with twenty-three jumps, held at the end of May at Auteuil racecourse.

745 The Grand Prix de Paris

First run in 1863, the Grand Prix de Paris started as a two-mile race; in 1986 the distance was reduced to 2,000 meters. The race is held at the end of June at Longchamp.

746 Phar Lap

Of humble breeding and background, Phar Lap, known as "the Red Terror" and "the Australian Wonder Horse," was a beloved figure in the 1930s in Australia and New Zealand during the Great Depression in Australia. He won thirty-seven of fifty-one starts.

747 The Dubai World Cup

Held in November in Dubai, the United Arab Emirates, the Dubai World Cup is the wealthiest race card in the world, with purses of $1 and $2 million, but no parimutuel betting.

TROTTING TO THE FINISH

In 1802, a coalition of religious groups was strong enough to force legislation closing all racetracks throughout New England, as well as the eastern seaboard states. However, racing continued because trotting, according to the courts, was not racing; racing implied competitive horses going their fastest in an effort to come in first. Trotting was a relaxed gait, and obviously a trotter was not going as fast as he could. Even in competition he was not racing. This afforded anti-reform New Englanders the "out" they needed, and trotting and pacing flourished in these sections of the country, particularly in the absence of flat racing, which was outlawed.

—Luigi Gianoli, *Horses and Horsemanship Through the Ages*

THE BIG FOUR IN HARNESS RACING;
OR, THE GRAND CIRCUIT

748 The Dexter Cup
The first step of the trip to the Hambletonian, the Dexter is a stakes race for three-year-old trotters, held at Freehold Raceway, Freehold, New Jersey, in early May.

749 The Hambletonian
A race for three-year-old standardbreds, the Hambletonian is the first leg of the trotting Triple Crown. Originally run in Goshen, New York, the race moved to Du Quoin, Illinois, for many years and is now held at the Meadowlands Racetrack in New Jersey in early August.

750 The Yonkers Trot
The second leg of the harness-racing Triple Crown. This stakes race for three-year-old trotters is held at Yonkers Raceway, New York, in late August.

751 The Kentucky Futurity
The final leg of the Triple Crown for three-year-old trotters, held at the Red Mile in Lexington, Kentucky, in September.

LADY SUFFOLK   ZACHARY TAYLOR   TACONY   MAC

THE PACING TRIPLE CROWN

752 The Cane Pace
The first leg of the Triple Crown of pacing, held on Labor Day at the oldest half-mile track in America, Freehold Raceway in Freehold, New Jersey.

753 The Little Brown Jug
The second leg of the pacing Triple Crown takes places at the county fairgrounds in Delaware, Ohio, the third Thursday after Labor Day.

754 The Messenger Stakes
The most prestigious pacing race, this finale to the Triple Crown was held at Roosevelt Raceway in New York City until that track closed. The race, owned by Yonkers Raceway, has moved from track to track in recent years.

Celebrated American Trotting Horses, painted by R. A. Clarke, 1854

JACK ROSSITER LADY MONSOON FLORA TEMPLE HIGHLAND MAID

HAMBLETONIAN
(1849–1876)

The grandson of the English sire Messenger, Hambletonian, by Abdallah, out of the Charles Kent Mare, sired 1,331 foals; almost all trotters and pacers racing today can be traced back directly to him.

A large, very muscular bay, Hambletonian was born in 1849 in Sugar Loaf, New York. He launched his stud career at age two, when he covered four mares.

Another son of Abdallah, Abdallah Chief, was thought by his owner to be the better of the two, so a challenge race was set. The two owners hitched their stallions to skeleton wagons at Long Island's Union Course. Hambletonian won, but Abdallah Chief's owner still insisted he had the better horse, so a time trial was held. Each horse trotted the track separately, Abdallah Chief doing a mile in 2:55 1/2, and Hambletonian clocking in at 2:28 1/2. This earned Hambletonian a reputation as a sire for speed, and his stud fee was set as high as $500. Some of his most famous descendants are George Wilkes, Dexter, Maud S., Greyhound, Lou Dillon, and Tagliabue.

Hambletonian died in 1876 at the age of 27. The Hambletonian Society formed in 1924 to promote trotting horses, and launched the Hambletonian Stake to honor the greatest sire in harness-racing history. The first Hambletonian was held in Syracuse in 1926. Today the race is held at the Meadowlands in New Jersey.

Rysdyk's Hambletonian,
painted by J. H. Wright, 1865

756 Lady Suffolk

The famed "old gray mare" in the traditional American song, Lady Suffolk began her career pulling an oyster cart and went on to set the world record for the mile as a trotter.

757 Lou Dillon

The "Queen of Trotting," this mare set a record for the mile in 1903, trotting the distance in 1:58 1/2.

758 Uhlan

Set the record for the mile in 1:58 in 1912.

759 Peter Manning

Lowered the record time for a mile to 1:56 3/4 in 1922.

760 Greyhound ("the Grey Ghost")

Set a new record for the mile twice in 1938; his fastest time was 1:55 1/4.

Lady Suffolk, 1849

Dean Hanover and Alma Sheppard

The Hanover Shoe Farm was a premier stable in harness racing, owned by Lawrence and Charlotte Sheppard. In 1937 they allowed their eleven-year-old daughter Alma to drive the sulky for the time trial of their top trotter, Dean Hanover. To everyone's astonishment, Alma set the world speed record for a woman driver, at 1:58 1/2 for the mile.

HANOVER SHOE
FARMS

FAMOUS PACERS

762 Messenger (1780–1808)

A direct descendant of the Darley Arabian, Messenger, an English gray Thoroughbred brought to the United States in 1788, is the founding sire of all standardbreds. Messenger sired many Thoroughbred racehorses—his descendants include Man O'War and Whirlaway—but his particular strength was in siring trotters and pacers. His most important contribution to the standardbred breed was his son Abdallah, who sired Hambletonian.

763 Dan Patch

Set world records for the mile in 1903, 1904, and 1905.

764 Bret Hanover

Setting the record for the mile in 1966, Bret Hanover was named Horse of the Year by the U.S. Trotting Association and the U.S. Harness Writers Association in 1964, 1965, and 1966.

765 Sleepy Tom

A pacer who set the world speed record in Chicago in 1879, Sleepy Tom was blind due to harsh treatment in his early days.

PUBLISHED BY CURRIER & IVES

The Pac

Wonder **SLEEPY TOM,** the Blind Horse,
RECORD 2:12¼.

Kathleen Adams with her adopted
Thoroughbred, Nine Ways

Retirement, Rescue, and Adoption Programs

Some racing Thoroughbreds that don't make the mark, or are retired, suffer a grim fate. Several organizations help racehorses, and other neglected horses, find better homes.

766 CANTER (Communication Alliance to Network Thoroughbred Ex-Racers)
Founded in Michigan, this organization now facilitates adoption of retired Thoroughbreds in six states.

767 Lost & Found Horse Rescue
This organization, based in York, Pennsylvania, rescues and places Thoroughbreds, as well as other breeds.

768 New Vocations
In addition to placing Thoroughbreds and standardbreds for adoption, New Vocations, located in Hilliard, Ohio, runs an outreach equine program for "at risk" youth.

769 Rerun
Rerun recycles ex-racehorses through reconditioning, training, and proper placement, in eight states.

770 Thoroughbred Retirement Foundation
Based in Shrewsbury, New Jersey, and the Kentucky Horse Park in Lexington, Kentucky, this is the largest humane organization dedicated to the rescue of racehorses.

771 United Pegasus
Dedicated to rescuing and placing the foals of mares bred to produce Premarin, a drug extracted from pregnant mares' urine, United Pegasus lobbies for legislation for better treatment of the mares, and provides education about Premarin alternatives. It is based in California.

In the Company

OF HORSES

SUMMER

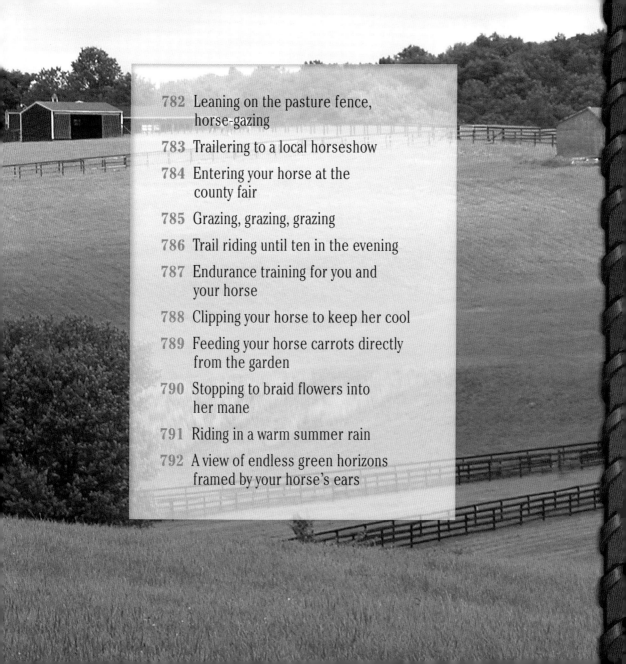

FALL

793 Wearing
Newmarket boots

794 Waxed jackets with
side vents

795 Knowing the hay is already baled
and stacked

796 Picking out the last cocklebur in
your horse's tail

797 Plucking an apple off the tree
for your horse

798 Feeling snug in a down exercise vest

799 Trail riding through orange
and red leaves

800 Soft fuzz beginning to grow on
your horse's legs

801 Putting away the fly masks and
getting out the rugs

802 Filling the bins with golden grain

803 Sorrels and bays
against fall colors

804 Horses getting frisky
in cooler weather

805
An autumn
pack trip in the
mountains

806 Not having to urge your horse into a canter

807 Fleece saddle pads

808 Harrowing the arena for rainy days

809 Riding in a comfortable sweater and jods

810 Tossing heads and manes in the breeze

811 Sharing a Kahlua and coffee after a ride with a friend

812 Talking to the farrier about winter shoes

813 Barn cats asleep in the waning sunlight

814 The crunch of leaves under a horse's hooves

815 Making every riding day count

Winter

816 A thick winter coat on you and your horse

817 Hoofprints in fresh snow

818 Water tank heaters

819 Box stalls with Christmas stockings tied to the doors

820 Taking a sleigh ride through powdery snow

821 Knee-high golden straw in stalls

822 Warm winter jodhpurs

823 Combing icicles from luxuriant manes

824 Enormous eyes with snow in their lashes

825 A horse's breath sending out a plume of white vapor as he whinnies

826 The howl of the wind outside a sheltered arena

827 Rolling in powdery snow

828 Chasing invisible wind spirits

829 Standing in line, rumps to the wind

830 Colorful horse blankets

831
White horses on a
white landscape

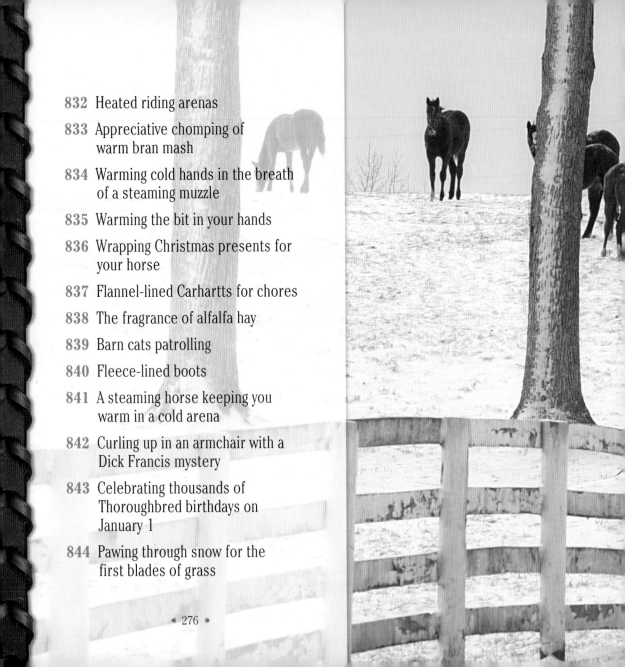

889 Giving your horse a massage

890 Knowing when to call the vet

891 Being welcomed by a whinny as you head toward the barn

892 Finding your horse with no new nicks or bruises

893 Finding a gopher hole in your pasture before your horse does

894 When your horse allows you to join him in a ride

895 Seeing the barn cat carry a squeaking mouse away from the barn

896 Soft lips taking oats from your palm

897 Bringing the horses in for the night

898 A brand-new, shiny pitchfork

899 A barn that's more orderly than your home

900 A clean, crystal-clear water tank

901 Your horse offering his foot for cleaning

902
Having a horse as one of
your best friends

903 Learning the Tellington Touch

A method developed by Linda Tellington-Jones to restore harmony and wholeness and modify the behavior of your horse through a series of exercises and body work.

904 "Joining up" with your horse

A technique popular with followers of the "natural horsemanship" training methods, in which you ask a horse to move around you in a round pen until it exhibits the submissive herd behavior of lowering its head and licking its lips, and turns to face you. The "join-up" is complete when you can step forward to pat the horse, turn your back, and walk toward the center of the pen, and the horse follows you as its leader.

THE LURE OF THE TACK SHOP

905 Going to the tack shop to buy a rubber band for your safety stirrup and coming home with new brushes, molasses horse treats, and a new pair of gloves

906 Being able to talk about your horse while you shop

907 Buying a present for your favorite riding companion

908 The overwhelming aroma of new leather

909 Sliding your calves effortlessly into a pair of tall, black, leather riding boots

910 Feeling the sudden need for a well-tailored riding vest

911 Having a name plate engraved for your horse's halter

912 A bridle with silver inlay

913 Soft woven lead ropes

914 Getting a tack store gift certificate for your birthday

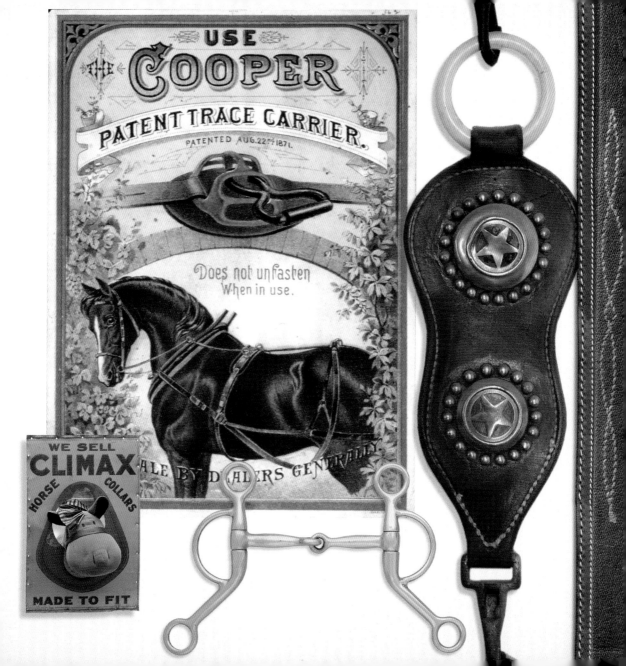

5/A EXTRA TEST.

This blanket stands the highest test for strength. It is in fast color

922
Finding the perfect blanket to suit your horse's personality

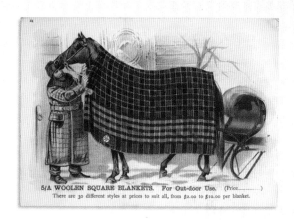

5/A WOOLEN SQUARE BLANKETS. For Out-door Use. (Price.............)
There are 30 different styles at prices to suit all, from $2.00 to $10.00 per blanket.

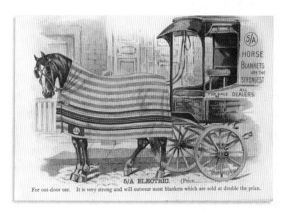

5/A ELECTRIC. (Price.............)
For out-door use. It is very strong and will outwear most blankets which are sold at double the price.

5/A FIVE MILE HORSE BLANKET. (Price.............)
This is the strongest blanket made at the price. Each blanket has Five Miles of warp threads.

ce.......................)

may be washed when soiled.

FRANK MILLER'S HARNESS SOAP

HORSE COMMUNICATION

947
Clever Hans

Clever Hans lived in the early 1900s. His owner, a gentleman named Herr Wilhelm von Osten, claimed to have a horse of extraordinary intelligence and set out to teach him to think, read, and count. Clever Hans could answer yes-or-no questions with movements of his head. Using an abacus with his nose and tapping out the alphabet with his hoof, Hans answered questions about geography, mathematics, music, and politics.

As Hans's reputation grew, so did the skepticism of the scientific world. In 1904 a group of learned men from various branches of science gathered to put Hans to the test. They, too, were amazed by Hans but knew he could not be accomplishing these feats alone; Von Osten had to be giving him imperceptible signs. Finally the scientists asked Herr von Osten to leave the premises. When they continued to ask Hans questions, the horse couldn't answer.

Clever Hans is often cited in texts on behavioral psychology as an example of "false intelligence," yet he was actually a very smart horse who responded to his master's subtle body language.

948
GREAT HORSE BOOKS

Black Beauty by Anna Sewell

Smokey the Cowhorse by Will James

Horse Heaven by Jane Smiley

Misty of Chincoteague by Marguerite Henry

The Black Stallion series by Walter Farley

Old Bones by Mildred Mastin Pace

Billy and Blaze by C. W. Anderson

Saratoga Backtalk by Stephen Dobyns

The Red Pony by John Steinbeck

Dick Francis's racing mysteries

My Friend Flicka by Mary O'Hara

National Velvet by Enid Bagnold

Seabiscuit: An American Legend by Laura Hillenbrandt

Cut Throat by Lyndon Stacey

On the Art of Horsemanship by Xenophon

The Race for the Triple Crown by Joe Drape

The Horse Traders by Steven Crist

Secretariat by Bill Nack

Horse People by Michael Korda

A Good Horse is Never a Bad Color by Mark Rashid

Wild about Horses by Lawrence Scanlan

Horse of a Different Color by Jim Squires

Lyons on Horses by John Lyons

The Man Who Listens to Horses by Monty Roberts

A Year at the Races by Jane Smiley

Dressage: The Art of Classical Riding by Sylvia Loch

My Horses, My Teachers by Alois Podhajsky

Classic Horse Movies

Seabiscuit (2003)

The Story of Seabiscuit (1949)

Spirit, Stallion of the Cimarron (2002)

Hidalgo (2003)

The Black Stallion (1979)

My Brother Talks to Horses (1946)

Miracle of the White Stallions (1963)

Phar Lap (1984)

International Velvet (1978)

The Great Dan Patch (1949)

My Friend Flicka (1943)

The Red Pony (1949)

A Day at the Races (1937)

The Horse Whisperer (1998)

National Velvet (1944)

The Misfits (1961)

I'd horsewhip you if
I had a horse.

—Groucho Marx in
Horsefeathers, 1932

950
Horses teach us the rewards
of patience and trust

Joys of Riding

951 Keeping up with your big sister

952 The clip-clop of hooves

953 Hacking out

954 Wool tweed riding jackets

955 Learning the proper riding aids

956 Feeling your mount respond to the lightest of nudges

957 Galloping on a racetrack

958 Leather riding gloves

959 A well-ridden half-halt

960 Riding in a parade

961 The exhilaration of the gallop

962 Taking a stone from your horse's foot

963 Straddling the broad back of a draft horse

964 Your horse not shying the third time you pass that scary tree

965 Foot warmers in tall leather boots

966 Loping through a meadow

967 Finding a fallen log in the woods that makes a perfect jump

968 Swimming your horse through a river

969 Riding at dawn

970 Riding at sunset

971 Casting long, late-afternoon, horse shadows

972 Centered riding

973 Surrender and trust

974 Balance

975 Riding as an act of faith

976 Trailering your horse to the mountains

977 Schooling your horse to the music
of a Viennese waltz

978 Facing a four-foot jump

979 The oneness of horse and rider

No hour of life is
wasted that is spen
in the saddle.

—Sir Winston Churchill

980
Riding under a
full moon

981
Inheriting your mother's
passion for riding

In riding a horse, we borrow freedom.
—Helen Thompson

999
With horses, we face
our fears and find
our courage

CHAMPION LADY BUCKAROO.

1000
Through horses, we discover
our gentleness and
our strength

There is no secret so close
as that between horse and rider

—R.S. Surtees